HER ST

Chosen

WOMEN'S MINISTRIES
PENTECOSTAL CHURCH OF GOD

HER STORY: CHOSEN Devotional, the HER STORY series, vol. 1.
Annual Devotional by Empowered Women's Ministries of the Pentecostal Church of God,
2701 Brown Trail, Suite 500, Bedford, Texas 76021—pcg.org/women

Editor in Chief: Kimberly Ming
Editors: Melissa Patillo, Stephanie Wheeler, Kathy Whited
Design and Layout: Department of Women's Ministries and Kimberly Ming
Layout Editor: Spencer Ming

Printed in the United States of America by Kindle Publishing

First Printing, January 2022

www.pcg.org/women

ISBN: 9798784111654

HER STORY: *Chosen*

The **HER STORY** Series
Volume One

EMPOWERED WOMEN'S MINISTRIES
PENTECOSTAL CHURCH OF GOD

pcg.org/women

HOW TO USE THIS BOOK

HER STORY: CHOSSEN is designed to be versatile and easy to use. When delving into these studies, you will find there are multiple ways to apply the information!

This can be read as a personal Bible study or used to mentor another woman. You can go through it informally with friends. Or it could easily be utilized as the curriculum for a small group, since it is designed complete with discussion questions. The chapter outlines lend well to also making it easy to use in large group settings for topical teaching or preaching.

The timeline is also flexible: It can be a 12-day (once a day), 12-week (once a week), or 12-month (once a month) study guide!

This beautifully designed devotional study book includes twelve devotions (Her Story) on women of the Bible that you will love, and there are twelve themed topics and key Scripture verses. Each session also includes:

- *Your Story: Personal Reflection* – Following each devotion, you will find personal application questions that will reflect back to what you just read.

- *His Story: Digging Deeper* – For those that want a deeper understanding of what the Word of God says on the given topic, this *"His Story: Digging Deeper"* section leads the reader on a journey into Scripture and questions of the text.

- *Simplify: Personal Application*– A personal challenge to help apply what has been learned.

- *Supplication: Prayer*– At the end of each chapter there is an applicational prayer.

- *Story Board: Journal*– Apply what has been learned through prayer. Don't forget what you've learned and what the Holy Spirit has been saying to you. There is plenty of space to journal those heart felt thoughts at the end of each session.

The margins in this devotional are wide so you have plenty of space to answer questions, write out thoughts or Scripture, and/or add your own creative doodle artwork.

We ask that you think about using this devotional as a resource to pour into another woman or a group of women. This devotional will also serve as a great gift for a friend, your pastor's wife, a missionary, or most importantly– an outreach tool to win and mentor the lost.

To order more, CONTACT us at:
empoweredwmin@pcg.org or
PCG.org/women

We dedicate this book

to all of the

Chosen Women of God,

past and present,

who lived out their

purpose,

and whose stories

have helped to make

*our **stories** stronger!*

This book belongs to a Chosen Woman of God:

_____

Place your name here.

TABLE OF CONTENTS

INTRODUCTION FROM THE DIRECTOR

I am excited to present this impactful study of twelve women in the Bible who were CHOSEN by God. For years I have had the dream to provide a quality, in-depth, women's study concerning the women of the Bible. When I read Scripture, I am constantly overwhelmed by women who were brave and strong and who made cultural differences for their times. So, I am overjoyed to release this very important and life-transforming message.

This devotional guide is a beautiful study of twelve women of the Bible who were chosen by God to walk out their divine purpose. Just like any group of women that might be put in a room together, these women are very different in personality, age, culture, and purpose. Some are well known while others are obscure. Some have glorious stories to tell full of love, romance, and success, while the stories of others are tragic and actually downright gruesome.

During this study, you will read the story of one of the most well-known or "Chosen" women of the Bible —Mary the mother of Jesus. You will also study the narratives of women much older and wiser than Mary who were established teachers (Priscilla), leaders (Deborah), grandmothers (Lois), and even disciples (The Women at the Cross). Yes, there were women disciples, and they followed Jesus to the cross and beyond.

Some of the women are childhood favorites like Hannah, Ruth and the Samaritan woman. Others may have names you don't recognize but are still exciting to get to know, like Achsah, Jael, or the Isaiah 54 Mother. The stories that you will read in the following pages are not fictional tales but stories of real women. They certainly had real experiences and struggles just like we do today, but they also had real encounters with a Holy God that changed their lives and purpose forever. God chose them so that His glory would be revealed through them to all the world. *"But you are God's chosen treasure… He did this so that you would broadcast His glorious wonders throughout the world"* (I Peter 2:9 TPT).

Like the women of the Bible, God has chosen you and me as His daughters, and with great love He has an appointed purpose for each of our lives. *"You have not chosen Me, but I have chosen you and I have appointed and placed and purposefully planted you, so that you would go and bear fruit"* (John 15:16 AMP). He has purposed that we do not sit idle or remain silent, but that we become fruitful trees, sharing the amazing stories of who He is and all that He has done. Your story becomes your greatest testimony of the goodness and wonder of God.

Chosen sister, as you read through the stories in this book (stories of Biblical characters voiced from our amazing authors), don't place your focus on the women. Doing so can become a comparison game. That is not what this book is about! But instead, pray that your eyes will be open to see the awe-inspiring character of God in each story. His role is center stage. His overwhelming love, compassion, and forgiveness provide the real message that needs to be heard. These are true stories of God's faithfulness to His chosen daughters for all-time. As you carefully read each page and search the Word, my hope is that you will discover that what God did in and through these women, He will do in and through you! **YOU ARE CHOSEN WITH A PURPOSE!**

Kimberly Ming Empowered Women's Ministries Director

ABOUT THE CONTRIBUTORS:

Amy Stoehr is a joyful worshipper, minister, mother of five, and grandmother of Olivia. She and her husband, Matthew, serve as the founding pastors (35 years) of The River Family Church in San Diego, CA. Her passion is prayer. She is involved in leading, teaching and mobilizing prayer teams around the globe. Matt and Amy have stewarded the vision of building River Gardens for events from spiritual impact to weddings and community events. She enjoys continually discovering the treasures of God's Word, time with family, engaging in Kingdom assignments, long walks in God's beautiful creation and great coffee.

Tami Miller loves Jesus and loves people. She has been married to the love of her life, Ted, for twenty-seven years and lives in Arlington, Texas. She has raised three wonderful children that make her proud to be their mom! Tami and Ted were lead pastors for twenty-five-years. She finds joy in teaching, leading worship, and building teams. Currently, God has directed the Millers to use their calling in the marketplace and to serve pastors nationally and globally. Tami always enjoys friends, walks, music, shopping, and a great piece of chocolate.

Margret Cox is the director of Women's Ministries of Northern California/Nevada. Alongside her husband, they serve as District Bishops and Assistant Generals of the PCG SW Division. Her passion has always been ministry, to women. She loves to share her story and encourage others through humor and love. She has been married for 50 years, and to-gether they have been blessed with 3 children, a daughter-in-love, a son-in-law, 11 grandchildren, and 4 great grandchildren. Some of her favorite things are traveling, preaching, loving new people.

Stephanie Wheeler is a wife, mom, dog mom, minister, and friend. She is an ordained minister with the PCG and a former Messenger College student. Stephanie and her husband Doug have been married since 1990. They currently serve as Lead Pastors of Freedom Christian Center in Manteca, California, and Northern California District Secretary. They have two grown children, Eric, and Rebecca, who also serve in church ministry. She loves connecting with friends and family, whether it's over a Bible Study or sitting in a coffee shop with her favorite latte.

Melissa Patillo and her husband of 29 years, Jimmy, pastor New Life Church in Frankfort, KY. She is an ordained minister and holds a B.A. in Biblical Theology and a M.A. in Theology. She has served as Academic Director for Life Christian University of KY, and, more recently, she served as the Kentucky District Director for the International Convention of Faith Ministries. Melissa has ministered nationally and internationally through her gifts of teaching and music. She is passionate about God's Word and presence, enjoys coffee and working in the cosmetology industry for the last 26 years.

Hope Reynolds serves as the Women's Ministry Director of the PCG Capital District. She is married, David, and they have served in pastoral ministry for 40+ years. For 33 years Hope traveled the world with her husband as David served as a USAF chaplain. Hope has a degree as a Radiological Technologist. She practices God's love for the "entire person"- body, soul, and spirit. Together they have four married sons and seven grandchildren and serve the PCG as Bishop of the Capital District, the Endorser of Chaplains, and Pastors of Victory Tabernacle in Maryland.

Andrea Dunn Is a passionate preacher, teacher, and worship leader. She is an ordained minister of the PCG and currently pastors Trinity Upper Room in New York, along with her husband. Andrea is a graduate of the Caribbean Pentecostal College in Jamaica where she earned a diploma in Christian Ministry. She is also a graduate of Springfield College in Maryland where she earned a M.A. in Social work. Andrea has a passion for women's ministry and has been engaged in empowering women through women's conferences, retreats and support groups.

Allison Smallwood serves as the Missions and Outreach Pastor at New Hope Church in Concord, California. Together with her husband, Mike, they have over 20 years of ministry experience reaching all ages and generations. Allison is passionate to see the lost get found and the found equipped to build the Kingdom. She is mom to five amazing kids, Noni to two grandbabies, and will never turn away a good cup of coffee or an opportunity to enjoy the outdoors.

Olivia Carter is 28 years old and currently lives in Fort Worth, Texas. She works as an Enrollment Coach for Concordia University. In 2017, she graduated from Messenger College with a B.A. in Christian Ministries with a concentration in Biblical Studies and, in May of 2020, she completed a M.A. in Theological Studies with a con-centration in Old Testament from the Assemblies of God Theological Seminary.

Kathy Whited loves to serve Jesus in ministry. She is currently a part-time Chaplain at a local hospital. She is pursuing a B.A. in Bible and Theology at Global University and is an ordained PCG minister. Her passions include leading worship, preaching, loving people, and reading God's Word! Kathy and her husband have served in ministry in many different capacities and are so thankful for every opportunity the Lord provides. Kathy loves her husband, children, and grand-children and she loves to bake homemade pies and rolls. (Check out her recipes in the back of the book- Yummm).

Susan Dawn Coffman has spent the last 45 years pastoring alongside her husband, Murvin. She is a PCG credentialed minister who loves teaching, training, and leading women in their walk with Christ, and preaching at women's conferences. She has dedicated her life to the joy of serving others inside the church walls as well as on the streets of her community. She and her husband are senior pastors in Salinas, California. Her caring personality and strong love for God have helped shape her to be the wife, mother, grandmother, and minister that she is today.

Ashley Sharp is on the pastoral team at New Life Church in Frankfort, Kentucky. She is a licensed minister, and holds a Bachelor's degree in Theology and a certificate in Women's Leadership. She is also a successful businesswoman, having been a self-employed licensed Cosmetologist for several years. She is a passionate preacher with substance, and loves to minister in dance. Having experienced the adverse affects of a broken home, and personal struggles in her teens, Ashley desires to see women experience spiritual freedom in every area of their lives.

Kimberly Ming is the National Director of Empowered Women's Ministries for the Pentecostal Church of God. She has a heart to encourage others to passionately pursue a relationship with God and find their purpose where they have been placed. She is an ordained minister with the PCG and a graduate of Messenger College with a B.A. in Biblical Studies/Pastoral Theology. She has served along side her husband as lead-pastors, as a District Women's Ministries Director, and as the assistant to two PCG General Secretaries. Kimberly has been married to her husband, Dr. Wayman Ming Jr., for thirty two years. He currently serves as the General Bishop of the PCG, and together, they reside in Fort Worth, Texas, and have a 18 year old   daughter, two married sons, and a very special grandson.

OTHER CONTENT CONTRIBUTORS-

Tia David is a Messenger College Alumni with a B.A. in Biblical Studies, Leadership and Administration. She is the Empowered Women's Ministries Assistant, and well as the event planner for the Pentecostal Church of God International Missions Center. She is also a licensed minister in the PCG. She is married to her husband Jonathan who has his own wood working business. Some of her passions include summer camp, remodeling furniture, and taking care of her two adorable cats. However, her biggest passion is spreading the love of Jesus.

Michaela Dove graduated with a B.S. in Christian Ministry and Music from Emmanuel College, GA, and is working toward her M.A. in Organizational Leadership. She is currently employed at Messenger College in Enrollment Services and serves as the Residence Director for the student body. She is a licensed minister in the PCG, she serves at Messenger College as the worship leader, and is involved in ministry through her local church. In her spare time, she enjoys the outdoors, visiting new coffee shops in the area, and learning different skills and hobbies.

WITH A SPECIAL THANK YOU TO:
Melissa Patillo, Stephanie Wheeler, and Kathy Whited who served with Kimberly Ming on the *Empowered Women's Resource: 2022 Devotional Book Development Team.* Your prayers, invested time, creative ideas, writing and editing skills, theological understanding and passionate study of the Word have brought a deep impact to this work. –KM

*"You have not **chosen** Me, but I have **chosen** you and I have appointed and placed and **purposefully** planted you, so that you would go and bear fruit..."*

- John 15:16 (AMP)

Chosen

TO
ARISE!

HER STORY

Deborah

By Amy Stoehr

"In the days of Shamgar son of Anath, in the days of Jael, the highways were abandoned; travelers took to winding paths. Villagers in Israel would not fight; they held back until I, **Deborah, arose, until I arose, a mother in Israel."**
JUDGES 5:6,7 (NIV)

Five years ago, I stood frozen in my parent's home in North Carolina, where I had come to help my dad care for my precious mama who was battling late-stage Alzheimers. I was trying to process what I was hearing on the phone through the desperate voice of our 22-year-old son's friend Wesley who was 2,400 miles away. *"Mrs. Stoehr, we don't know what to do. Jon is out of his mind, He just peeled out of here in his truck and he is saying that he can't take any more and that he is going to end his life tonight. Please, please, we have to find him. I saw it in his eyes, he is serious."* You can imagine the immediate fear that tried to envelope me as my mind started to race. The Holy Spirit spoke to me so clearly in that moment- *"Remember I am with you, I am with Jon. Trust Me, stand on my Word and Arise my beloved."* I knew what He meant, and I asked Him to help me. Through that fateful choice to trust, stand and arise in God, the Lord saved our son from ending his life. He rescued him from the enemy's grip; set him on a new course of authentic relationship with Him; and gave him a heart like Caleb to influence his generation. We are so thankful. That was when I began to learn more about Deborah and how to position myself in His presence to "Arise" to God's purposes.

A HEARING EAR

Judges 4:4 tells us that as a prophetess and judge, Deborah could be found regularly under a specific palm tree between Ramah and Bethel in the Mountains of Ephraim. The Israelites would line up to counsel with her and the Lord would give her His wisdom and revelation concerning them. She had such a reputation that a tree was named after her—The "Palm Tree of Deborah."

> ## She would have to ascend into the presence of God in order to bring wisdom and justice to God's people.

Notice her location: She was positioned between *Ramah* and *Bethel*. "*Ramah*" means *"ascending heights,"* and "*Bethel*" means *"House of God"* or *"Presence of God."* She was positioned between "ascending the heights" and "the presence of God." As a judge, she would have to ascend into the presence of God in order to bring wisdom and justice to God's people.

A WORD FROM GOD

On a particular day, she heard a Word from the Lord that propelled her into action. The cry of His people had come to Him and He spoke to His beloved Deborah, who had a "hearing ear" and it changed the course of a nation. Obeying God, Deborah called Barak to his destiny. He said "*yes*," but would go *only if Deborah went with him.* He recognized that victory could only happen with the Lord's presence, and he knew Deborah heard from God. Because of this, the honor of the battle would go to a woman instead of him. Nevertheless, they partnered together.

Barak obeyed the command from the Lord (Judges 4:6-7). When Canaanite commander Sisera heard this, he gathered all his 900 chariots, horsemen, and warriors and marched toward the Kishon River Valley. Judges 5:8 (NKJV) lets us know that Israel had *NO WEAPONS!* They had not been training because they were basically enslaved. You can imagine how they must have felt as they stood looking down at the highly equipped vast army of warriors in all of their glistening iron of the chariots! However, they had Barak, Deborah, and a word from the Lord!

A VICTORY WON

At the appointed time God told Deborah, *"Arise! Today the Lord will give you victory over Sisera, for the Lord is marching ahead of you!"* (Judges 4:14 NKJV) The battle commenced! With every step they ran closer to those who had held them in captivity for 20 years. They did not draw back or hesitate, but *boldly trusted in the Word of the Lord* through Deborah and the Lord wrought a great victory that day! We read in Judges 5:19-22 that the Brook Kishon came as a flash flood and pushed the enemies back, killing many of them, while Sisera fled on foot to the house of Jael. It was where he would meet his death with her tent peg! (*Read more about Jael's story in "HER STORY: Chosen" Chapter 8*).

For the next 40 years of Deborah's time as a judge, God's people were delivered from bondage, and lived in peace! We see in Judges 5 where Deborah is looking back to the great victory the Lord has orchestrated. She and Barak are praising the Lord together, recounting God's hand of deliverance for His people! It was because of their obedience and the obedience of those who joined them. I love verse 2 (NLT), *"When Israel's leaders take charge, and the people gladly follow—bless the Lord!"* The moment it all began to turn around was when Deborah took her place as a chosen woman of God: *"Village life ceased, it ceased in Israel, Until I, Deborah, arose, Arose a mother in Israel."* Judges 5:7 NKJV

LIFE LESSONS:

1. **A HEARING EAR:** You may be experiencing a challenging season that seems overwhelming. You may be facing disappointment, hopelessness, unmet expectations, heartbreak, betrayal, or failure and feel like life, as it used to be has ceased...But all is not lost! When you are desperate to see a divine turn-around it's time to arise! We arise by crying out to God for His intervention! We arise by having a *hearing ear* to the Spirit of God! We arise by taking our place in the authority He has given to us as His daughters in His matchless Name! Do you have a hearing ear in the middle of your challenging situation?

"The whole earth waits in eager expectation for the sons and daughters of God to arise." Romans 8:19 NKJV

2. **A WORD FROM GOD:** When we are positioned daily in His presence, in the secret place, our abiding in Him will give us His eternal perspective. Learn to wait on the Lord. Deborah was familiar with His presence, *knew His voice* and was obedient to His leading. She took great delight in obeying Him and trusted fully in Him. As you abide in Him and fellowship with Him, you will learn to hear His voice for yourself. Posture yourself to hear Him. You will find the answers that you need to all of life's questions. You will also find that He is walking with you every step of the way. A *hearing ear* will enable you to receive *a Word from God!*

3. **A VICTORY WON:** Deborah saw the daunting enemy, but at the appointed time she obeyed the word from God and she charged! She knew the natural facts, but trusted in God's faithfulness! She knew the odds, but she proclaimed, *"Arise! Arise Barack*!" God is calling you to *arise* and spring into action! Just like Deborah, you cannot play it safe or hold back! When you get a word from the Lord, run into the battle with courage that comes from your surrender to the Lord, and you will find victory every time! As you choose to *AWAKE*, *ARISE*, and *GO IN HIS NAME*, the knowledge of the glory of the Lord will cover the earth as the waters cover the sea (Habakkuk 2:14)! You will be amazed at how far reaching your victory will be!

YOUR STORY: Personal Reflection

God called Deborah to a unique assignment and He supplied her with His grace, wisdom, and power. He is still calling Deborahs to arise and take their place. Think higher, expect bigger and throw off limitations as you position yourself in the presence of the Lord, as she did, waiting upon Him in prayer and worship. Daily attention to His Word is key. The Lord will use your unique relationship with Him to position you in just the right place at just the right time.

Read Judges 4:5

When God called her, Deborah was positioned between Ramah *"ascending the heights of prayer"* and Bethel *"House of the Lord"*. She had a reputation as a woman who spent time with God and spoke His word. Her life-style was saturated with the presence of God. She was as close as she could be to Him. This closeness was not just to bless her life; it was to prepare her for her chosen moment. She knit herself to God through prayer and worship.

Read John 15:1-17

Is there a connection between "abiding" and "arising"? Explain.

According to this passage what will our lives produce if we abide in Jesus?

God will use our position in Him to position us to influence others. Chosen Woman, you are a vessel of influence. You connect as you relate. Fill out the box below.

WHO I AM:	WHO I INFLUENCE:
MENTOR/LEADER	
WIFE	
MOTHER	
CO-WORKER	
FRIEND	
PRAYER WARRIOR	
WORSHIPPER	

Read Romans 12:9-21

Becoming a vessel of influence is a weighty position. We must not take it lightly.

According to the above verses, List the qualifications of such a woman.

-
-
-
-
-
-

Read Isaiah 60:1-3

Times may be dark, but God is still calling Deborah's.

What is the result of a chosen woman answering the call to arise?

Write a petition to the Lord for abiding and arising based on John 15 and Isaiah 60:1-3, (The following scriptures may inspire you: Jeremiah 29:13, Psalm 25:1, Philippians 3:13-15, James 1:5).

SCRIPTURE REFERENCES: Read Her Story!
Judges 4 and 5

SIGNATURE:
DEBORAH [DEB-uh-rah: "Honey bee"- prophetess and judge of Israel]

SETTING:
[Date: About 1300 B.C.] Deborah was the fourth of twelve judges of Israel. The Canaanites had been ruling harshly over the Israelites for 20 years. It was a dark time. It was a continual cycle of disobedience, correction from the Lord, the people crying out for help, and the Lord sending a judge to deliver them. God's people lamented and cried out to Him and God sent a woman to arise– Deborah.

Dear one, I believe our Beloved has chosen you to be a Deborah in our time. Though your specific assignment is unique to you, and can only be completed by you, you are part of a great company of women called to proclaim the Good News and see the Kingdom of God advance in the Earth. He will give wisdom and courage, ignite faith, baptize you afresh in His love and expand your vision beyond your natural thinking.

Don't allow any circumstance to become a limitation.

Read Judges 5:6-7 – "A Mother in Israel"

In Hebrew,

"MOTHER IN ISRAEL" is *"Shakamti",*
which means *"healing and mending."*

Isn't that a beautiful description of women who answer the call? Every one of us is chosen to serve in this capacity. You are fully equipped to serve in this way.

Read 1 Corinthians 12:1-11 & 27 and Ephesians 4:11.
List all the ways the Holy Spirit calls and equips us to serve.

According to Ephesians 4:12, why are we called and equipped?

Read Galatians 5:22-23. Fill in the heart below:
- **Inside of the heart write all of the ways you feel called or gifted to serve**, (This is not a natural talent list; it is solely based on the Scriptures).
- **Around the outside of the heart list the fruit that you can bear according to the above Scripture.**

As we step into our role as a "mother", Christ's character abounds and flows from our lives. God called, and Deborah arose. She walked in her position as "*Shakamti.*" Because of this, she was able lead Barak and walk in God's divine purpose for her life.

Read Judges 4:14-16

How did the battle end for Barak that day?

Read Judges 5:12 ESV. Fill in the blank.

> "Awake, awake, Deborah! Awake, awake, break out in a song
> _____ Barak, _____ _____
> _____!

Clarke's Commentary describes the above verse with this comment; *"Make those captive who have formerly captivated us."*

Read 2 Corinthians 10:5.

Not every army marches around you, some enemies need to be destroyed within. When you inspire greatness, you never know the magnitude of victory it will bring someone.

What are we taking captive according to the above verse?

Chosen woman, your walk will always impact your relationships. When you allow the Holy Spirit to flow in your life, He will draw greatness out of those around you.

Read Hebrews 10:24

List seven ways (one for every day of the week) **that you can stir another to good works and greatness.** (Refer to your "heart" full of Spirit-given gifts).

1.

2.

3.

4.

5.

6.

7.

Chosen daughter, you have everything you need. Never feel you are at a disadvantage. Don't compare yourself but inspire and be inspired by those around you. The Lord has called you now arise!

See how the Lord has provided for your mission. He has given you:

- **THE HOLY SPIRIT:** Unlike Deborah, you don't just dwell near the Lord, He dwells IN you! If you have received Jesus as Your Savior, trusted Him as Your Lord and have been born again as a new creation in Christ (John 3, Romans 3:23, 6:23, 10:9,10, and Romans 5:8)) the Holy Spirit came to live inside you.

- **THE WORD:** Deborah did not have access to Jesus' Words! She did not have a Bible. But you have continual access to God's living Word, the Bible. It is your daily Bread, Your Foundation, Your Treasure, Your Weapon.

- **THE CHURCH:** You have the empowering strength of a whole army of Empowered Sisters who are locked arm in arm in agreement to see God's purposes come to pass in our time. Link arms with them. Link arms with them and run alongside to the fight. The power of our unity is exponential.

Read the following scriptures and put an "X" in the box that the verse describes. Some verses may have more than one.

Scripture	The Holy Spirit	The Word	The Church
Psalm 119:105			
John 15:26			
Philippians 4:2			
Acts 1:8			
Ephesians 4:11			
Ephesians 6:18			
Romans 8:16			
Ephesians 2:13			
Matthew 4:4			

Fun Facts: About Deborah and Other Things

- **Deborah** (Deborah, D'vorah in Hebrew) is translated "honey bee": Bees are one of God's most remarkable creatures. They follow their leader. Their sting is painful, but their honey is quite sweet. Bees are busy collecting pollen and nectar, not for their own benefit only, but for the benefit of others.

- **Barak**: means "lightening rod." A lightening rod becomes powerful when it is activated! Barak was activated to his destiny as Deborah called him to arise, then came alongside him in his assignment. And so, he also arose, and he was empowered to call ten thousand others together.

- **Mount Tabor**: 10,000 Israelites ran down the one-mile slope of Mount Tabor. It is still a one-mile slope today! At the base of the slope was the Brook Kishon (Kishon Valley).

- **Kishon River**: flows from the mountains of Galilee to the Mediterranean Sea. Also the site of Elijah's slaughter of the 450 prophets of Baal in 1 Kings 18. Later in history, Napoleon watched the Arab army be decimated by a flash flood in this very place of the Kishon valley that God had planned for a set up ambush of Sisera's 900 iron chariots which were pushed back as far as the Mediterranean Sea by the flood of the Kishon.

- **Ramah:** heights, ascending the heights (Deborah's Palm Tree that she sat under was positioned between Ramah and Bethel)

- **Bethel**: House of God, presence of God

- **Significance of the Palm Tree**: Deborah sat under the Palm of Deborah. Palms are an emblem of Justice. The people could come freely to meet with Deborah there.

- **Deborah's Song**– Deborah is only one of three women in the Old Testament to have a poem ascribed to her. Found in Judges 5, this poem is considered one of the oldest texts in the Old Testament, possibly dating back to the twelfth century BC.

SIMPLIFY: Personal Application

I challenge you my sister to be desperate for the presence of God and to obey Him in every way.

- Consecrate yourself in surrender to Him daily- repenting of sin, deception and distractions, not being lukewarm, but ignited by His fire and becoming known as a burning torch of His presence among the sheaves of the nations (Zechariah 12:6).

- Love God's Word- develop a warrior mentality to use this Sword of the Spirit as the Lord has intended and declare His Word taking authority over every form of darkness in the Name of Jesus.

- Live from a place of abiding fullness– Drink of His presence, listen to His voice. Let Him fill up your heart and direct your purpose.

- Learn to wait on the Lord and live in Him as a branch to the vine.

- Make worship and praising Him your lifestyle– Delight in Him for He delights in YOU.

After studying the story of Deborah, how will you posture your heart and ears to hear and obey the voice of the Lord?

A hearing ear will enable you to receive a Word from God!

-Amy Stoehr

SUPPLICATION: Prayer Focus

Father, I adore You. Thank You for choosing me and for positioning me in Your Light as Your daughter and a new creation in You. I humble myself and present my heart to You. I thank You for Your living Word, may it come alive in me. Give me Your perspective to see beyond my own circumstances, to see the harvest fields. Help me to become a chosen daughter who arises by positioning myself in Your presence, speaking Your Word with power, and not shrinking back against the enemy. Give me a renewed passion for loving others. Empower me to carry Your presence every day. Thank You for Your Grace to Arise In the purpose that you created for me. In the matchless Name of Jesus ,
Amen.

STORY BOARD: Journal Notes

What was revealed to you about the Character of God through HER STORY?

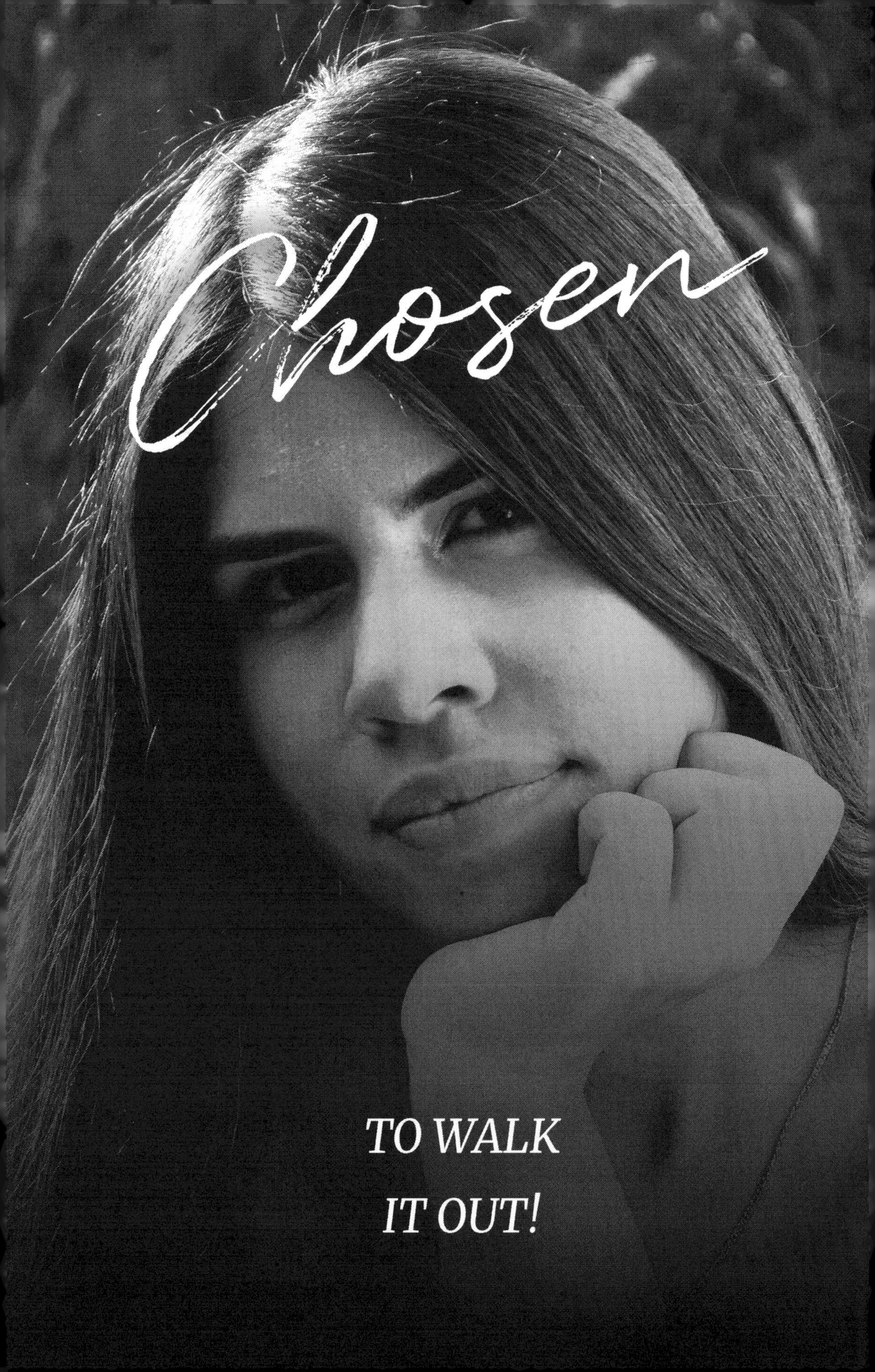
Chosen
TO WALK
IT OUT!

HER STORY

Ruth

By Tami Miller

*"Again, they cried openly. Orpah kissed her mother-in-law good-bye; but Ruth embraced her and held on. Naomi said, 'Look, your sister-in-law is going back home to live with her own people and gods; go with her.' But Ruth said, 'Don't force me to leave you; don't make me go home. **Where you go, I go**; and where you live, I'll live. Your people are my people, your God is my god; where you die, I'll die, and that's where I'll be buried, so help me God—not even death itself is going to come between us!'"*

RUTH 1:14-17 (MSG)

Do you ever feel like things haven't quite gone as you planned? I think we all start off with big dreams and a perfect plan. We try to follow all the rules. I mean really trying to do everything right. This was me. I grew up in a Pastors home and was saved and called by God at a very young age. In fact, I remember my mom telling me, "Tami, you are never too young for God to use!" I took this to heart. I was ten years old at the time. I began pursuing God, seeking to know His voice and trying to discover His plan for my life.

Everything changed two years later when I was told my Dad had a moral failure. The repercussions this had on our family, the church, and our whole life was astronomical. We were all so angry, hurt, and disappointed but this was not the end! This was the beginning. There are two people that changed my life: A repentant dad and a forgiving mom. They were willing to walk this out together. The restoration process for us was long and hard but it has made me who I am today, for this I am grateful. Our stories are never over when we think they are. Neither was Ruth's.

Our stories are never over when we think they are.

Ruth. Moabitess. Marries a Jewish man. This family she has married into serves a different God than her family. They have different customs, different celebrations, and different practices of worship. One thing is clear, they love their God, Yahweh, and He is good.

WALKING THROUGH THE UNPLANNED

The plan was to get married, have children, and live happily ever after.

Ruth got married….

Her husband died….

She had no children.

This is not what she had planned! She had Naomi. Her friend. Her mother-in-law. Oh, how Ruth loved Naomi! She had taught Ruth the ways of Yahweh and His people. She had shown her true kindness and love. On the road to a new place, grieving but holding on to the one true relationship she had left in this world-Naomi told her to go home. Naomi used to be pleasant, now she was bitter. She had lost her husband and both of her sons, and she was blaming her God. It must have been like slow motion to Ruth's eyes as Orpah, her sister-in-law (the only person who had truly walked in her shoes) kissed Naomi goodbye. She watched her walk away with tears of finality and remorse streaming down her face. This was a lot of loss! First, her father-in-law died, her brother-in-law died, her husband died, and at that moment her sister-in-law was walking away from the family! Then Naomi stepped up to hug Ruth goodbye but Ruth held on to her refusing to let her go! This was the moment that Ruth realized, bitter or not,

Naomi was her family and she would not leave her. Nothing would separate them unless it was death, and she said as much. Naomi's family was now her family. This God that Naomi loved yet blamed, was good, and He would now become her God too. She refused to succumb to grief and make a decision to part from the only true friend and mother that she had. She chose to go with her. She chose to walk this out with Naomi. Ruth declared, *"Don't force me to leave you; don't make me go home. Where you go, I go; and where you live, I will live. Your people are my people, your God is my God; where you die, I* will *die, and that's where I will be buried, so help me God—not even death itself is going to come between us!"* Ruth 1:16-17 (MSG)

WALKING THROUGH NEW TERRITORY

Upon arrival following a long journey, Ruth didn't know what to expect. She had just left everything she ever knew. She had just been through great loss, what would her future look like? Would these Israelites embrace her or reject her? The people seemed nice to Naomi but leery of her. What would be the next step? She know that it would be harvest season soon, and the harvesters always left the extras for the poor. Ruth decided to go and gather from what was left. This could have been dangerous for a single, young woman. After all, where would she go? She had no idea. Her safety and direction were left to Yahweh. She headed out alone, just putting one foot in front of the other. Trusting and afraid. Overcoming fear, she was just walking it out!

Walking through new territory, Ruth had no idea whose field she would end up in. All she knew was that the field owner, Boaz, saw her, asked about her, spoke to her, and blessed her. He offered for her to work solely in his fields with his workers, who he instructed to leave extra grain for Ruth to harvest, which would make her job easier. This provided Ruth with safety and security. He even invited her to eat lunch with them and took notice of her at the table. When Ruth returned home after her first day of work, Naomi asked whose fields she harvested from and who had been so generous to her. After telling Naomi it was Boaz, Naomi explained that he was a kinsman redeemer- a close relative that could take responsibility for all that was Elimelech's, including Ruth's hand in marriage and the hope of carrying on the family name. Overcoming fear had worked in her favor!

WALKING THROUGH THE UNKNOWN

After harvesting season was over, Naomi came up with a plan for Ruth to let Boaz know that she was available and willing to marry him. Remember, the Israelite customs were foreign to Ruth. However, she followed every detail of the plan including laying at his feet on the threshing floor. Would he accept her? Would he be upset that she was there? How would he react? These were all unknowns! When he awoke, Ruth told him who she was and that she was willing to marry him. Boaz assured her that he would take her as his wife and that he was honored to do so. There was just one obstacle, there was a younger, closer kinsmen redeemer than himself. He would have to go to the city gate and negotiate with him concerning Ruth. Would she be handed over to a stranger? Would he be as kind as Boaz? What would her future look like? She would have to overcome the unknown again and wait for Yahweh to work it out.

Boaz left no stone unturned. He took care of all the legalities and married Ruth in the proper way. Boaz and Ruth conceived a son. They named him Obed. Obed is the father of Jesse, the grandfather of David, King of Israel. God worked behind the scenes in Ruth's life, ordering every step to bring her from a desperate situation to blessing. Overcoming every obstacle that life threw at her was, and still is, a beautiful testament to the goodness of God!

Ruth. Moabitess. Widow. Daughter to Naomi. Wife to Boaz. Mother to Obed. Grandmother to King David. Ancestor to Jesus the Messiah.

LIFE LESSONS:

1. **WALKING THROUGH THE UNPLANNED:** Has life ever thrown you a curve ball? Have you ever dreamed of your life being one way, but it turned out another? Loss comes from a lot of sources— loss of a job, loss of relationships, divorce, death. Loss is life altering. It can shake you to your core. If you live long enough, loss comes. The proper handling of our loss is vital. When life is bleakest, we must remember hope is not lost. Things may never be the same, but life can be good again. There is a God of all comfort (2 Corinthians 1:3, 4) who comes to us at these times. We need each other. Throughout my childhood hardships our extended family and friends made all the difference. They provided a support system to help us see restoration. Restoration in the Kingdom isn't when things are put back in their original state but instead, they are made new and better. This is my testimony!

2. **WALKING NEW TERRITORY**: Often when we don't know what our next step will be it causes fear and anxiety to come. Especially if we have been through loss! Questions arise: How will I make it? What do I do now? An important reminder is to keep walking! Keep putting one foot in front of the other. These are times we live moment by moment in the strength of God. We don't have to figure it all out right away! The Bible states, "Fear not" 366 times. That is one "fear not" for every day of the year plus Leap Year! Remember, the Greater One lives on the inside of you (1 John 4:4)! Trust Him! Rest in Him. There's no need to fear anything that life throws at you because He is with you! New territory comes after loss and it can be an exciting time when you put your Hand in the Master's hand!

3. **WALKING THROUGH THE UNKNOWN**: It's one thing to overcome fear after a tragedy, it's another thing to walk in confidence into an unknown future! Our posture tells a lot about us. Growing up I always heard, "Stand up straight, shoulders back." Our spiritual posture is just as important. It must be one of trust. Trusting an unknown future to a known God! Psalm 37:23 (NKJV) states, "*The steps of a good man are ordered by the Lord, and He delights in his way.*" Know that God has a plan. Trust Him with every step! The old hymn says, "Jesus, Jesus, how I trust Him, how I've proved Him Oe'r and Oe'r. Jesus, Jesus, precious Jesus. Oh, for grace to trust Him more!" The same God that was with you in the past, is the same God who is with you now. The same God that is with you now is the same God who will be with you until you draw your last breath! You can trust your future to a God like that!

YOUR STORY: Personal Reflection

Cartoonist Allen Saunders once quipped, *"Life is what happens to us while we are making other plans."* The writer of Proverbs expresses this sentiment a bit differently: *"In their heart humans plan their course, but the LORD establishes their steps" (Proverbs 16:9 NIV).* God designed us with a mind and will to choose our path and make our choices. He knows what happens next and He knows what's happening now. Don't worry; He has you right where you need to be. Chosen Woman you are a daughter of the Most-High.

Waiting is also a type of walking. Waiting can be an undefined space that the enemy tries to use to stop the growing process in your life. Waiting can cause doubt.

List three thoughts you struggle with the most when waiting on God.

    1.

    2.

    3.

Looking at the circle graph below, consider your answers.

1. **Fill in the graph by sections according to which solution you are most likely to do,** *(for example, you may struggle with believing the lie that *you are not good enough*).*

2. **Shade in the graph according to how much you personally struggle** (It may be 40, 50 or 60 percent). Everyone's graph will look different. Fill in your percentage of struggle with all three thoughts from above. It will help if you have colored pencils or pens so you can see the different portions clearly.

STRUGGLES

Now list three practices that foster trust in the waiting.

    1.

    2.

    3.

Do the same thing with this graph. This time your answers are based on what you would put into practice as you waited. It could be "see council" or "pray more." You know your personality, only you can answer for you. Be honest, this is a great evaluation tool.

STRENGTHS

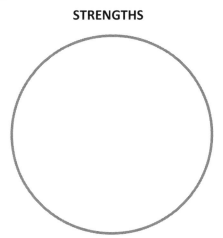

Compare the two graphs; often a visual aid will help us see where we need to trust God to grow us in a certain area.

How does your graph of struggles compare to your graph of strengths?

Certain life-events/unforeseen circumstances will compete for our attention and seek priority in our lives. Life can challenge us to question our identity as daughters of God. We must resist any pressure to conform to a thought or opinion that does not agree with our identity in Christ.

Make a short list of the events in your life, large or small, that have caused you to question your identity as a child (Daughter) of God.

Fill in the following statements with truths from His Word. The first one is done for you.

1. I was discarded, but now I am *GOD'S CHOSEN TREASURE.* **1 Peter 2:9 TPT**

2. I was an orphan, but now I am _____

    _____. **2 Corinthians 6:18**

3. I was lacking, but now I am _____

    _____. **Colossians 2:10**

4. I was isolated from God, but now I am_____

    _____. **Ephesians 2:13**

5. I was walking by sight, but now I am _____

    _____. **2 Corinthians 5:7**

You may add your own declarations to this list, it is infinite.

HIS STORY: Digging Deeper

SCRIPTURE REFERENCE: Read Her Story!
Book of Ruth Chapters 1-4, Matthew 1:5

SIGNATURE:
RUTH [ROOTH: unknown exactly- Thought to be from the word *reuth*, which may either be the word for "something worth seeing" or the word for "friendship" or "female friend"]. Both meanings of the name were true of Ruth.

SETTING:
[Date: Around 1100 B.C.] The life of Ruth occurs during the period of the judges, between the death of Joshua and the rise of Samuel's influence. It is thought by Jewish tradition to be written by Samuel, but the author is unknown. This was a time of spiritual confusion and moral decline. There is a famine in Bethlehem Judah that caused Elimelech to move his family; wife, Naomi, and two sons, Mahlon and Chlion, to Moab. Elimelech dies in Moab. Then Mahlon and Chilion marry Moab women, Orpah and Ruth. After 10 years, Mahlon and Chilion die leaving Naomi, Orpah, and Ruth all widows. Naomi hears that the famine in Bethlehem Judah is over and decides that it is time to return home.

Jesus came on the scene and changed our story, just like Boaz did for Ruth. He laid down his life to redeem us from our sin and shame and rose again to victory claiming us as His! He took responsibility for us in order to carry on His family name. Jesus sees us, provides for us, and protects us. He is kind and generous and blesses us. Jesus reminds us who He says we are. He takes care of business; he is our Kinsman Redeemer. He gives us His name, His bloodline. He walks it out with us. We are His daughters!

Fill in the blanks from 1 John 3:1a (NLT).

See how very much our _____ loves us, for he calls us His _____, and that is what we are!

Peter in Prison

Read Acts 12
Peter was chosen to walk out a life-event, but he wasn't walking alone. The future was unsure, but the Lord was guiding their steps.

How secure was Peter imprisoned?

The night before his trial what was Peter doing and why is this important?

The Lord sent an angel to help Peter. What were the angels' first instructions to Peter and what happened immediately following?

Why do you think the angel gave such detailed instructions at Peter's deliverance?

Read over the story. How many soldiers, and how many gates and guard posts did Peter pass?

_____ Soldiers   _____ Gates and Guard Posts

The odds are never so high against us that the Lord can't cause us to walk through. When He chooses a path for you, He provides the help you need to walk through it.

Pray today and ask the Lord to open your eyes to His activity in your trials.

What did Peter find the church doing when he arrived at Mary's home?

What happens to us affects others, what we do on behalf of others affects them.

 What do you do when a "walk-it-out" season becomes a full-on desperate run, then and a collapse?

 You turn to the Scriptures and see how the Lord helped others in desperate situations.

The Shunammite Woman
Read 2 Kings 4:8-37

When Elisha prophesied about the birth of her child, what was the Shunammite woman's reaction?

Why do you think she responded the way she did?

Do you truly feel the Lord is guiding your steps, establishing your way?

Read on and see what "the Lord guiding your steps" could look like.

When the Shunammite left her home and arrived at the Elisha's she replied to both her husband and the prophet's servant Gehazi the same way. Her words have been immortalized in a hymn that bears the same.

Compare the two passages.

Verse 23 (NKJV)- *"So he (her husband) said, 'Why are you going to him (Elisha) today? It is neither the New Moon nor Sabbath'. And she said, 'It is well'."*

Verse 26 (NKJV)- *"Please run now to meet her, and say to her, 'Is it well with you? Is it well with your husband? Is it well with the child?' And she answered, 'It is well'."*

She had opportunities to speak out of a broken heart. Her words could have been filled with anguish but each time she chose to acknowledge the goodness of God. He was guiding her steps and her steps brought her to the lowest point any mother could reach. Still, she chose to walk forward trusting God.

Take a moment to put yourself in her place. Study her words and imagine her heart. What can you learn from her behavior in this crisis and how can you apply it to your walk with God?

Note: she refused to leave the man of God. She walked in step with him back to her home. We know her story ended in victory but remember, she was living it out. She did not know what the sunset of that day would bring but she positioned herself to her source of blessing and would not move off her confession of goodness.

Do you tend to move away from God when it looks like things are headed to a bad end?

Why is it a natural inclination to withdraw from the source of all goodness when things are dark and painful?

I like to remind myself, "If it's not good, God's not finished yet!" Since my child-hood, I have walked through many more hurts and disappointments. I have lost a child. Both of my parents. What I thought was a lifetime ministry path. Many friends. The list could go on; as I am sure you have a list of your own. What do we do with it? The loss? We keep walking it out. We trust God, especially with what we do not understand. We trust Him with our question marks. All of our loss does not compare to the goodness and love of God. He walks it out with us.

Read 2 Corinthians 4:7-9

What is the Lord's promise to us in this passage?

List the problem and the promise for each scenario mentioned in verse 8 in the box below.

PROBLEM	PROMISE

They say, "When life gives you lemons, make lemonade." I'm not sure who "they" are, but what I do know is that there is something to this saying. Scripture tells us over and over that God is good. Our culture is doing everything it can to prove that wrong. In fact, this lie started in the Garden of Eden with Eve and the serpent. *(Read Genesis 3). One way to combat this lie, is to make declarations over your life, from Scripture. It is important to make these declarations out loud.

Read Romans 8:31-39
Let's declare:

> *"God loves me so much that He gave His only Son. His love for me is so strong that nothing can separate me from it. There is no circumstance that I will face that will keep His love from me, we are inseparable. God is on my side; He is for me. No matter what I see or hear around me I know that God is good, and His love is unmatched. I declare today that I am loved and accepted by God and nothing and no one can separate us! I am His and He is mine!"*

Our situation does not change who God is, instead it gives opportunity for Him to prove it over and over again.

Ruth is an example of living in the sovereignty of God with an open heart and open hands. Her story began as a wife, widow, sister, and daughter. She had no idea the path that God would choose for her to walk, but she walked as dutifully as she could. She took steps to go beyond where she ever imagined herself. She took steps to walk along side of her widowed mother-in-law as she bore her own grief and pain. She took steps and leaps trusting in a God that she didn't even really know, and God blessed her with divine connections along the way. She remained committed and teachable in her relationships. We would do well to learn from her story.

Reflect on a time when you experienced healing and or restoration through a God given relationship. Were you the "Ruth" or the "Naomi"?

We all have most likely all walked out the role of both women in our relationships, and because the Lord is guiding our steps, neither role is more important than the other. What counts is your obedience to trust in Him.

Fun Facts: About Ruth

- The Lord redeemed her genealogical line. She came from the Moabites. Moab was conceived in sin (Genesis 19:30-38 NKJV) but the Lord brought redemption.

- There was purposeful provision provided for her and Naomi. (Ruth 2:16 NKJV)

- Ruth's vow (1:16-17) is used in many wedding ceremonies today.

SIMPLIFY: Personal Application

As we have looked at Ruth's life and God's sovereignty in it, I hope you are encouraged in your life story. God is with you and He is good. If you are in the middle of loss, heartache, or disappointment, your story is not over! Keep walking it out. If you have come out of loss, heartache, or disappointments with so many questions, trust God with your question mark and keep walking it out. Knowing that He is GOOD! It is not just something that He does, GOOD is who He is.

- *Think of a particular present situation that is troubling you.*
- *Write it down.* This might be written here, on a different piece of paper that you tuck away somewhere, or in a personal journal where you write those things that the Lord is speaking to you.
- *Pray over it.* Release it to God while you wait on the Lord's resolve to come.
- *Wait while you walk it out.* Trust our GOOD God especially with the question marks!

SUPPLICATION: Prayer Focus

Father, Thank you for giving Jesus to walk it out for me, all the way to the cross. Thank you for raising Him to life so that I can live an abundant life in You. Thank you for sending Holy Spirit to be with me always. I surrender my past, all the things that I do not understand, and wish were different. I trust You with my future. You know better than I do, and You work all things out for my good. You are God, I am not! Just as You have chosen me to walk it out, I choose to walk it out with You! I love you and I trust you!
In Jesus Name. Amen.

STORY BOARD: Journal Notes

What was revealed to you about the Character of God through HER STORY?

Chosen

TO ASK
FOR MORE!

HER STORY

Achsah

By Margret Cox

"Then Caleb said, "Whoever attacks Kirjath Sepher and takes it, to him I will give my daughter Achsah as wife. And Othniel, the son of Kenaz, Caleb's younger brother, took it; so he gave him his daughter Achsah as a wife. Now it happened, when she came to him, that she urged him to ask her father for a field. And she dismounted from her donkey, and Caleb said to her, 'What do you wish?' So she said to him, 'Give me a blessing; since you have given me land in the South, give me also springs of water.' And Caleb gave her the upper springs and the lower springs."

JUDGES 1:12-15 (NKJ)

I love the relationship that Achsah had with her father. I never experienced that type of relationship with my own father. At a summer school camp, when I was around 8, they had a parents night dinner. I watched, with my little girl eyes, how a little girl ran into the arms of her daddy who swept her up with glee. I have never forgotten that longing as a child. My father was a violent man when he was drinking. I may not have been wanted by my earthly father,

47

but when I was born again, my heavenly Father prepared and designed a new relationship just for me! God's angels were rejoicing, "It's a girl!" Now, I go to Him with all confidence and love because He has my interest as His priority. I ask because I can! It is that simple.

No one can be you, but YOU!

There are so many heroines that God chose for His purpose in the Bible. But how many sermons have we heard about *Achsah*? She did make the book! God saw her as important enough to include her by name! No one can be you but you!

One of the meanings of Achsah's name is *ankle bracelet* or *tinkling ornament*. A bracelet encircles the wrist or ankle it is placed on, and I am sure she was a daddy's girl who had him encircled around her little finger! She was his only daughter, and from birth she was probably a tinkling sound he always heard coming. We are also God's daughters, and He loves to hear us coming as well. So, what can we learn from this unique woman of God named Achsah?

This little story of a daughter and her father is recorded twice in the Bible (Joshua 15:13-19; Judges 1:12-15). If God saw it important enough to have it inserted twice, He has a lesson for us to learn! Achsah's life is an example of a successful inquirer! In her story, we can glean principles of how to be a **successful inquirer** of our Heavenly Father!

HER ASSESSMENT
Achsah was a newlywed with an estate as a dowry. She looked the land over and immediately saw what was needed. She knew the land her father gave would be of little use without springs of water. She assessed the situation, then she went to him with a very definite request.

We learn from Achsah the principle of assessment. Before we utter one word of prayer, we need to assess, or *know exactly* what we need. 1 John 5:15 (KJV) states, "*And if we know that He hears us, whatsoever we ask, we know that we have the petitions that we desired of Him.*" The Greek word for *petitions* denotes *a specific, exact, precise, detailed request*. It is so comprehensive that it leaves no room for misunderstanding. This is exactly what Achsah did when she assessed her situation to prepare a detailed request from her father.

HER ASSURANCE OF FATHERS FAVOR

The second principle we glean from Achsah is to *have confidence in our Heavenly Father's favor*! The first thing out of her daddy's mouth was, "What can I do for you?" Caleb was a good father. And no good father hates to hear his child tell them what they want. Achsah knew it wasn't going to be a displeasure for her dad to hear her ask him anything!

Good fathers always show *liberality* in giving! It's their way of showing *favor*! Our Heavenly Father actually knows our needs before we pray (Matthew 6:8). But God's way of giving to us is through our asking. Prayer isn't designed to *inform* God, but to *activate our faith* in our loving Father whose good pleasure it is to *"give us the kingdom"* (Luke 12:32). Our Heavenly Father feels pleasure in giving His daughters all we need! By giving to us, God does not impoverish Heaven. God loves to give to us as the sun loves to shine! That's who He is! It's His nature! God has always been into scattering bounties among his children!

HER APPEAL

The next principle we see from Achsah is that she knew *exactly* what she wanted, and she knew *exactly* how to ask for it. She appealed to her father, "GIVE ME A BLESSING!" There is nothing wrong with that request! It is a good beginning! A father's blessing is an inheritance to a loving child. Achsah *knew exactly what she was asking for* and she was *very direct in her request*.

> **Ingratitude will seal up any spring of blessing. Grateful praise to our Heavenly Father will insure a future blessing or a present favor.**

It's important to note that her request was mingled with *gratitude!* She let him know she was *thankful* for the land he had already given. Ingratitude will seal up any spring of blessing. Grateful praise to our Heavenly Father will insure a future blessing or a present favor.

HER ACQUISITION

Achsah acquired what she asked for and more! Caleb gave her the upper springs *and* the lower springs! Are you even surprised? Why are we surprised at times when God blesses us with our petitions and more? The Word tells us that *God is able to do exceedingly, abundantly above all that we ask* (Ephesians 3:20).

Achsah provided us with a pattern. It is a good one. Don't miss it! She shows us how to confidently receive great blessings, just by asking and believing.

LIFE LESSONS:

Through the beautiful story of Achsah, we glean the following principles in how to be a successful inquirer of our Heavenly Father who gives liberally:

1. **ASSESS YOUR SITUATION.**

    a. Make sure you know the need, want, or desire.
    b. Make sure it is in line with His word or His will.

2. **BE ASSURED OF YOUR HEAVENLY FATHER'S FAVOR.**

    a. Know that He loves you.
    b. Know that He desires to give you good gifts.

3. **ASK CORRECTLY (APPEAL).**

    a. We must first be grateful for what we have been given.
    b. We must boldly ask in faith.

4. **RECEIVE FROM YOUR HEAVENLY FATHER (ACQUISITION).**

    a. It's one thing to know how to ask, it's another to know how to receive.
    b. Don't be surprised when you get exactly what you ask for and more!

YOUR STORY: Personal Reflection

No matter what season you may find yourself, there will always be needs. It is I mportant to understand that even though we are daughters of the Most High, we face many different seasons in our lives. But through every season, we will always have access to the same perfect, loving, and generous Father. He loves to bless His kids and has more than enough for every need! Even though He is omniscient (all-knowing), our Father requires us to approach Him with our petitions.

Have you ever wondered why?

One word: Relationship!

Our relationship with our Father is everything! He loves everything about you, even when you come to Him with your needs. When you consider this truth, it may change the way you approach His throne.

How do the following statements describe your relationship with your Heavenly Father? (1=NEVER AND 5=ALWAYS, circle the number that you identify with most.)

- I wake up with a desire to connect to my Heavenly Father.   1 2 3 4 5

- I make Bible reading and prayer a part of my morning.   1 2 3 4 5

- I only think about praying when I need something.   1 2 3 4 5

- I never ask His help with the little things in my day.   1 2 3 4 5

- I am mindful that He is with me all throughout the day.   1 2 3 4 5

- If my day begins to fall apart, my first thought is to ask Him for help.   1 2 3 4 5

- If I make mistakes or fail, I feel like my behavior changes God's attitude toward me.   1 2 3 4 5

- I end my day with connection and thanksgiving toward my Heavenly Father.   1 2 3 4 5

Based on your answers, how solid is your relationship with your Heavenly Father?

Do you go to Him for EVERY need big or small? Why or why not?

Sometimes we don't see the whole picture where God does! Have you ever asked God for something and didn't get it? How did that affect how you prayed for needs after that?

We often need to encourage ourselves by remembering the blessings God has given us.

Describe some of the prayers God has answered for you.

Read James 1:15 in The Passion Translation
"Every gift God freely gives us is good and perfect, streaming down from the Father of lights, who shines from the heavens with no hidden shadow or darkness and is never subject to change."

Consider this picture of your Heavenly Father, inviting you to His throne. He hides no part of Himself from you, He holds nothing back.

He is good.
He is perfect.
He is for you.
He has chosen you to ask for more!

How will this vision of Him, looking at you and listening to you EVERY time you come to Him, change the way you approach His throne?

SCRIPTURE REFERENCES: Read Her Story!
Joshua 15:13-19; Judges 1:12-15

SIGNATURE:
ACHSAH (ACK-sah= "anklet" or an ornament adorning the heel area.).

SETTING:
[About 1390 B.C.- During the conquest of Canaan]. Israel finds itself at a standstill as their leader, Joshua, has died. The people inquire direction from the Lord as to who will lead them now. Judah is appointed to fight the Canaanites. Caleb, who was once a spy of the Promised Land with Joshua, comes on the scene and offers as a prize his courageous daughter, Achsah, to the one who conquers a portion of the land.

The act of asking puts one in a vulnerable position. It requires trusting in the one we are asking. You may have a negative experience in this area from earthly relationships, but you must not allow that to define your relationship with your Heavenly Father. It is important that you have a correct understanding of who He is and how much he wants to bless you. Achsah knew she could trust her father to hear her petition and deal lovingly with her. Caleb didn't rebuke or accuse her of always coming or begging. He didn't tell her she already had enough given to her! She asked, and he was delighted to bless his daughter with even more! If you are a daughter of God, then you have an inheritance! May every woman go to her Father, just like Achsah went to Caleb.

Consider Hebrews 11:6
"And without faith it is impossible to please him, for whoever would draw near to God must believe that he exists and that he rewards those who seek him" (NLT).

According to this verse, if we desire to draw near to God, what two things must we do?

1.

2.

How important is it that the writer of Hebrews included the phrase "He rewards those who seek Him" in this passage?

We do not have a one-sided relationship with our Heavenly Father. It's true, our salvation is through faith in Jesus and there is nothing we can do to earn it. How-ever, once we are in relationship, we must maintain our responsibilities. Scriptures teaches that us we can have a father-daughter relationship with God (Romans 8:15). Remember, while every Bible verse regarding our relationship isn't about   asking and receiving, they have been inspired by God to cultivate the relationship He desires with us.

Look up the following passages and identify your responsibility and God's responsibility.

SCRIPTURE	Your Responsibility	God's Responsibility
Proverbs 3:5-6		
Matthew 6:33		
Matthew 11:28		
John 1:12		
1 John 1:9		
1 John 3:22		
1 John 5:14		

Do you see the pattern of generosity and faithfulness in the character of the Father? Yes / No

Whenever we feel we cannot approach the throne of God, we should remember who He is and how He feels about us.

Describe how God feels about you using the above scriptures and your answers from the "God's Responsibility" column.

PERCEPTION EQUALS REALITY
Let's compare Achsah's petition with another very familiar story.

Read Genesis 32:22-32.
Jacob's name means "heel grabber or schemer." He was used to getting his way through fraud, but in order for him to receive a blessing, a change had to come his way.

After decades of trying to solve his problems by lies and deception, Jacob was heading into an unknown future. While running from His troubles, he encountered a "man," who was the Lord, and spent the night wrestling with him. At the end of their encounter Jacob asked for a blessing and the Lord asked Jacob his name. No more schemes. Jacob faced the worst in himself and told Him his name. When he was honest and humble, God changed his name to Israel meaning *"One who strives with God."* Notice the blessing came after the relationship was established.

Achsah's name means "anklet" or an ornament adorning the heel area. She knew who she was standing in front of. The relationship was already established. She was a daughter, and she wasn't afraid to ask for what she needed for her future.

If you approach God feeling like you need to hide part of yourself from Him, you will be hindered. If you approach Him as a Father who loves you as His beloved child, your confidence will soar.

We often approach God based on who we are instead of who He is. Jacob was a deceiver, Achsah was a daughter. Both got blessed but Jacob had to come to terms with himself. Don't be afraid to approach God no matter what you think of yourself. God wants to bless the "heel grabber" and the "anklet" but they both must make their way to the throne. Perception equals reality, if you approach God feeling like you need to hide part of yourself from Him, you will be hindered. If you approach Him as a Father who loves you as His beloved child, your confidence will soar.

"Let us then approach God's throne of grace with confidence, so that we may receive mercy and find grace to help us in our time of need"
Hebrews 4:16 (NIV).

Do you have days when you feel more like Jacob than Achsah? What do you tell yourself when you feel like you can't approach the throne of God for help?

What prevents you from feeling bold in the presence of your Heavenly Father and how should we approach Him according to Hebrews 4:16?

Read Ephesians 3:20 (AMP)
"Now to Him who is able to [carry out His purpose and] do superabundantly more than all that we dare ask or think [infinitely beyond our greatest prayers, hopes, or dreams], according to His power that is at work within us..."

Achsah was given upper and lower springs on *"the sloping field"* (AMP). That meant her source would never run out. **Her father was positioning her for success. She would always have more than enough for the moment**. God desires to bless you with more than enough. In

Read Luke 6:38
What is the exciting declaration in this Scripture?

The Lord has many ways to give blessings to you. There is no shortage of abundance in His kingdom, all you have to do is ask.

Read Ephesians 3:20 as quoted above (Read it out loud several times if you need to and write it out a time or two to memorize it. Write it on a post it note and stick it on your mirror as a continual reminder of God's Faithful Word to you).

The Ephesians 3:20 verse is describing God's ability to bless and equip our lives. *Write down something you feel is lacking in your life. According to this verse what should you do about it and what more should you expect?*

Do you have enough confidence in God as your Father to ask Him confidently for your blessing? Why or Why not?

In Genesis chapter 17, the Lord appears to Abram and has a very important conversation with him.

Read Genesis 17:1-8. Keep in mind, Abram wanted an heir to inherit his wealth, the Lord had so much for in mind for him.

How does the Lord reveal Himself to Abram? What name does He use? What does that mean to you?

The Lord then changes Abram's name. What is his new name and what does it mean?

What does the Lord ask Abram to do in verse 1?

What would the Lord's command to Abram look like in your life? How would you live that out?

Your life may not seem as exciting as these Bible heroes and heroines but remember daughter of the Most High, you are just as loved and just as called to walk out each of these verses. If you are a mom, career girl, student, or any combination in your unique season of life and you have everything you need available to you from your Heavenly Father. He specializes in more-than-enough. Do not be afraid to ask and trust that you will receive.

SIMPLIFY: Personal Application

The challenge for you today is to pour out your heart to Him with all the boldness, confidence, simple ease and familiarity of a trustful and loving child. Bring to Him that need, concern or desire. This daughter was not fearful to go before her father. She did not dread asking him for anything because she knew him. **SHE WAS CHOSEN TO ASK FOR MORE!** We can see the way and the manner she went to her father. She was bold, confident, grateful, and straightforward. Then we see the way in which her father treated her—with abundant favor! He not only gave her one spring, he gave her two! Regardless of what our situation is or was with our earthly father, we have a Heavenly Father who loves, favors, and is generous toward His daughters! He wants us to ask Him for more! ASK, ASK, ASK, He wants you to ask Him for more!

What is it that you want to boldly ask your Heavenly Father for today?

Fun Fact: About Achsah

♦ ACHSAH's Name meant *"Ankle Bracelet or Tinkling ornament"*- Perhaps her father knew when she was coming by the sound she made. Our Heavenly Father hears the sounds we are making too. *What sounds are you making?*

SUPPLICATION: Prayer Focus

Lord, I thank You that You are the God of more than enough. Your resources are not limited! I ask You to help me to pray big; to believe big! You have chosen me to ask for more! As I look to You to supply all of my needs, help me to know that You desire to do exceedingly abundantly above all that I can ask, so I will keep asking for more! In Jesus name,
Amen

STORY BOARD: Journal Notes

What was revealed to you about the Character of God through HER STORY?

_____

_____

_____

_____

_____

_____

_____

_____

_____

_____

_____

_____

_____

_____

HER STORY

The Women at the Cross

By Stephanie Wheeler

"For I consider that the sufferings of this present time are not worth comparing with the glory that is to be revealed to us."
ROMANS 8:18 (ESV)

" Girls, I need your prayers." My phone lit up as I received this group-text on a cold February winter night. It was from my sister. It wasn't a prayer for aid with finances, sickness, trouble with neighbors or any of the usual needs of women. This was a desperate entreaty for perseverance. My sister was facing the worst pain and trial any mother, first-born son who was 33-year-old was dying. *"Girls, I need your prayers. My son is on the final leg of his journey, and I need the strength to see him through it."* Isn't that the true picture of mother-hood? The strength she was asking for was not for replenishment or reserve but to immediately flow into ministering to her child. She knew it would take everything she had. She expected to be empty when his journey was complete. But in the pause between contemplating what was before her and exhaling into the most heartbreaking task a woman can perform, she caught her breath and called out to her girls for support. Then...the most wonderful thing happened...

THE TRIBE

First, a little background. You see, in our family, we have an amazing tribe of women. We span three generations of the strongest ladies: aunties, cousins, grandmas, and sisters. We have walked through fire and difficulty. We have faced crisis and loss. We have laughed and cried and pledged ourselves to each other with unwavering support. A few months before that cold February night, we had taken a girls' trip. As with our previous trips, we gave each other small gifts of love. I always brought homemade goodies, others were more creative. On this particular trip one of the cousins gave each of us a pair of purple socks with our girl-trip theme printed on the bottom. We piled on the bed and laughed ourselves to tears trying to get a selfie, feet up in the air, showing off our socks.

Fast forward to February. As I sat there staring at my phone, searching my breaking heart for just the right words, a photo appeared in the group text. A simple photo from one of the girls. It was not of her face but her feet. She was wearing the socks. We sent photos of ourselves wearing our socks. The socks we had laughed over were now symbols of our commitment to walk our loved one through her worst days and hours—***our commitment to persevere!*** Not long after we would gather for the celebration of life for one far too young to be with Jesus. We cried. We hugged. I had the privilege of helping officiate the service. As I prepared and talked with my sister, she reflected on the account of Mary, mother of Jesus, at His crucifixion. The pain she must have endured losing her young man was not lost on her. It was not lost on me either. Mary had such a remarkable but ordinary life for the one assigned to birth the Messiah. She was a wife, a mother, and a friend. She was part of a community of friends, sisters, and cousins. It was at her darkest time that they were there with her. As Mary watched her son die for all humanity, she did not do so alone. There was a small band of women who stood by her with love, support, and tears. They were chosen by God to abide in that moment with her. These women were committed to walk with Mary through her worst days and hours. ***They were committed to persevere.***

> **These women were there with Mary until the end of that long, unimaginable day. They maintained their purpose and risked everything to walk with her.**

THE TRAGEDY

The word *PERSEVERE* is defined: *"To maintain a purpose in spite of opposition or discouragement; not to abandon what is undertaken."* I cannot think of a better description of the women at the cross. They are mentioned by all four gospel writers. These women faced such incredible opposition. They were outnumbered and unable to defend themselves; accompanied only by the disciple John. The scene at the cross was a combination of a riot and a massacre. I cannot imagine the sorrow mingled with chaos in Mary's heart. The only comfort she knew was in the tears and words of the women who stood with her. We don't know the exact number, but we know the group consisted of women who loved and followed Jesus. There was His mother, perhaps an aunt, the mother of James and John, as well as other friends or relations. They were there for Jesus, but they were also there for Mary. Doing life together was as natural as taking a breath. They had raised children, kept homes, seen miracles, and now stood together during an inconceivable tragedy that made no sense. These women were there with Mary until the end of that long, unimaginable day. They maintained their purpose and risked everything to walk with her. In other words, her girls had their socks on! Little did they know that a few days later their tears would turn to shouts of joy when Jesus rose from the grave and overcame for us all. This life only tells half the story. In God's kingdom the horrific can never compare to the triumphant.

THE TRIUMPH

We have all experienced trauma and harsh seasons. It is so hard to persevere when we *do* understand, but what about when we do *not*? In those moments when we are hit so hard and a "why" is all we can manage, we need comfort and encouragement. We need a tribe of women who will put their socks on and walk with us through the most difficult days. Paul says in 1 Corinthians 5:7, *"We walk by faith and not by sight."* Just because you don't understand doesn't mean you don't have to keep going. Perseverance is not popular and it's not pretty, but it is a necessary part of the believer's life. We have to encourage ourselves that this life only tells half the story. We don't know what is happening on the heaven-side of things. While you are persevering, Jesus is working in ways you don't see. A.W. Tozer said, *"While it looks like things are out of control, behind the scenes there is a God who has not surrendered His authority."* God has given you everything you need to persevere to the end. Chosen Woman, God has designed you to persevere with purpose!

Note: My sister still has the text thread from that night. It brings her great comfort to know in her worst moment, she had a loving tribe of women to walk through it with her. She keeps moving forward trusting the Lord with all heart, knowing my nephew is rejoicing in the presence of Jesus. We know that because one woman's son had to die another woman's son will live forever!

LIFE LESSONS:

1. **THE TRIBE**: Do you know your "tribe?" God doesn't want us to live our life in isolation. He has given us each other. It's important to have women around us who we trust and walk with us through the various seasons of our lives. This can be christian girlfriends, your women's group at church, or family members. If the mother of Jesus needed a tribe, we need a tribe! If you have unknowingly isolated yourself, make it a matter of prayer. It's important to know your tribe! Ecclesiastes 4:9-12 TPT states, *"Two are better than one, because they have a good reward for their labor. For if they fall, one will lift up his companion. But woe to him who is alone when he falls, for he has no one to help him up. Again, if two lie down together, they will keep warm; But how can one be warm alone? Though one may be overpowered by another, two can withstand him. And a threefold cord is not quickly broken."* Your tribe will help you persevere in the hardest of circumstances! That's just what we do!

2. **THE TRAGEDY**: Heartbreak, loss, and tragedy are a part of life. When they occur, it makes you feel as though your life is spinning out of control. Sometimes it's hard to keep calm in the chaos. When heartbreak, loss or tragedy strikes, it's vitally important that we are not alone in the persevering. In the natural, we have our tribe. In the supernatural, we have the Comforter, the Helper, the Holy Spirit. He alone can bring the peace and strength that we need to persevere through the hard times. When you have your tribe, and the Helper, you can make it through anything that life throws your way! Philippians 4:13 TPT states, *"...I find that the strength of Christ's explosive power infuses me to conquer every difficulty!"* Heartbreak, loss, and tragedy are not the end! There is a glory that will be revealed! It's coming! Hang in there!

3. **THE TRIUMPH**: Just because you don't understand the trial, doesn't mean you don't have to keep going. Perseverance is a part of our DNA as a believer! We have to encourage ourselves that this life only tells half the story. We see through a glass darkly (1 Corinthians 13:12). If we saw the heaven-side of things it would make things a lot easier. But this is where we must trust the One who knows and sees all! He sees the whole picture while we just see a part! God has given you everything you need to persevere to the end. Chosen Woman, God has designed you to persevere with purpose! He has triumphed. You will too!

YOUR STORY: Personal Reflection

STATEMENT OF FAITH

First things first. Before you get into the "My Story" portion of this study, I want to ask you a very important question. Have you started living "your story" in Christ? Are you born again? You can't persevere with purpose unless you recognize your primary purpose is to be in relationship with Jesus as Savior and Lord. Chosen Woman, your salvation is the most important part of this study. If you have not made that commitment, then pray this prayer with your group or by yourself:

Jesus, I _____ admit that I am a sinner and I cannot save or help myself in this condition. I believe the gospel story of your death as punishment for my sins and your resurrection for hope of eternal life. Forgive me and make me new. I confess you are Lord and Savior of my life now and forever, Amen.

Welcome to the family of God! You now endure with a **purpose**—to live out your story in Christ and impact your world for eternity.

Look at the definition of "persevere" as written in our devotion and fill in the blanks:

To maintain a purpose in spite of _____ or

_____ ; not to _____ what is undertaken.

Notice the definition itself seems to encourage us to remember two important things.
- ⇒ There will be resistance when walk in our God-given purpose.
- ⇒ Don't quit doing what God has given us to do.

In what areas of your relationship with Christ do you feel resistance or opposition?

Do you recognize opposition as a hinderance from the enemy or do you just feel like you are not destined to be an overcomer? Explain.

What do you do when you feel like giving up?

Let's break down that definition a little more. The concept of perseverance can be a little intimidating. If we better understand what it is to persevere, we will identify as a woman who is equipped in Christ to persevere with purpose.

*Do an internet search for "synonyms of persevere," (*any website such as dictionary.com or thesaurus.com will provide a list of words or phrases that help define "persevere.")

PERSEVERE=

Write down the word or phrase and an example of what that looks like in your life. (For example, "carry on" I faithfully attended my church even though I had been offended and the Lord strengthened me to forgive and walk in unity.)

1.

2.

3.

4.

The writer of Hebrews compares living our purpose in Christ to running a race. Runners must train and prepare their bodies for the race; we also must prepare our hearts and minds to run our race toward eternity.

In Hebrews 12:1 we are given this instruction:
"Therefore, since we are surrounded by such a great cloud of witnesses, let us throw off everything that hinders and the sin that so easily entangles. And let us run with perseverance the race marked out for us."

What are some things that keep you "tangled up" and hindered from running with perseverance?

Remember our sufferings and struggles are only half the story. Everything you endure in this life will make sense in glory. God is working all things for our good and He doesn't waste one moment of our lives in His plans. Don't get overwhelmed when you feel like you aren't making progress.

Read the following excerpt from a devotion entitled "Run the Race":

The Christian life is not a "just-try-harder" self-salvation project. It is all about what God has done, is doing, and will do in Christ by the Spirit. You have been created, blessed, and chosen for a purpose. You are not an accident. You are not a mistake. Your life matters because it is part of God's larger plans and purpose for the world. What's that purpose? In any and every season, to be God's beloved child and to live all of life for the praise of God's glory.

SCRIPTURE REFERENCES: Read their Story!
Matt. 27:55,56, Mark 15:40,41, Luke 23:49, John 19:25

SETTING:
[The Crucifixion, Jerusalem, Circa A.D. 33]—The sight of a first century Roman crucifixion was not for the faint of heart. Roman soldiers had great contempt for Jewish citizens and created the most humiliating ways of executing them. According to Josephus, Passover may have brought between one and two million visitors to the city. The political and religious manipulation surrounding Jesus' arrest created riot-like conditions. In the midst of this chaos, Mary, His mother, and a small group of women stood near, watching His pain and humiliation. Imagine the press of the crowds, the jeering voices mocking and cursing, the smell of His blood and sweat mingled with dust. Her sobs could only be heard by those who huddled nearby. It was the most important yet most horrific moment of all time.

"Why does God allow suffering?" It's probably the most asked question in Christendom. The truth is, we don't fully know because in this life we don't fully fathom the reasons why things happen. I like the phrase, *"This life only tells half the story,"* when considering suffering. To me it means there are things that happen here that won't make sense until we are fully glorified in heaven with Jesus. There is work done *here* that will be rewarded *there*. There are people we impact *here* that we will find out to what extent we did *there*. And, unfortunately, there are seasons, events, and traumas that we will endure *here* that we will only understand *there*.

We may not understand why we endure the things we go through, but we can go through them if we understand what the bible says about perseverance.

Consider our key verse Romans 8:18 (ESV).

> *"For I consider that the sufferings of this present time*
> *are not worth comparing with*
> *the glory that is to be revealed to us."*

Now consider the Greek translation:

- *"**CONSIDER**"*—Gr. *Logidzomi (*lo-gid'-zo-mi) — to compute or calculate. To studiously reach a conclusion.

- *"**SUFFERINGS**"*—Gr. *pathema* (path'-ey-ma) — that which one suffers or has suffered, externally or internally. This doesn't refer to generalized suffering in the human condition but our own *personal* pain and trauma.

- *"**GLORY**"*— Gr: doxa — The glory or majesty of God. All that He is.

- *"**REVEALED**"*—Gr. apokalupto *(Where we get our word apocalypse.)* — to uncover or make known.

Looking at these definitions, we can better understand what Paul was writing to the Roman believers.

To paraphrase: *"After giving much careful thought to all the terrible things I've suffered in this life, I have come to the conclusion that they cannot compare to the moment I will have a personal audience with the Most High God!"*

Chosen Woman, the joy that will be felt is not just about *seeing* God but *fellow-shipping* with Him forever. This understanding does not *diminish* our suffering but *empowers* us to persevere (*maintain our purpose in spite of resistance, opposition, or abandon what we have undertaken*).

Write your own paraphrase to Romans 8:18. Look up different versions to help you.

How do you think putting this key verse into your own words will empower you to persevere in difficult times?

Read 2 Peter 1:13.

"His divine power has given us everything we need for a godly life through our knowledge of Him who called us by His own glory and goodness."

Read that again.

The Word says you have everything you need to live a godly life. Everything? Yes, everything! Persevering isn't showing the world *your* power to live well, it is showing the world *God's* power to live well. We persevere by showing the world how Jesus would handle our situation. Jesus wanted to make sure we have everything we need to do that.

FOUR ESSENTIALS THE LORD HAS PLACED IN OUR LIVES TO EQUIP US TO PERSEVERE:

1. PURPOSE

Leonard Ravenhill said, *"Jesus did not come into the world to make bad men good. He came into the world to make dead men live!"* Salvation is more than a makeover. We are saved for a purpose. Persevering (*maintaining our purpose*) in hard times is possible when we understand what our purpose is.

Read 2 Timothy 1:9, 1 Peter 2:5,9,10.

Our purpose is unique, how we walk it out in Christ is described in the above verses. The Word of God is the same for all but works as instruction for each individual life.

Describe your purpose. Are you a businesswoman, educator, woman in ministry, stay at home mom?

What does it look like to be "a living stone" or a member of "the chosen generation" in your story?

2. PROVIDENCE

God is in control of everything. He revealed Himself in His Word as trustworthy and capable of handling our problems. I love that He did this even though He didn't have to. He tells us over and over again who He is and that we can depend on Him.

Read Romans 8:28; 11:36, and Colossians 1:15-17.

Think of a difficult time you endured. Was it hard for you to put your trust in the Lord to bring you through? Why or why not?

How would you use these verses to encourage another woman who was enduring a difficult time?

3. PRAYER and PRAISE

When King Jehoshaphat and King Hezekiah were faced with threats from their enemies, they called for prayer. God has given us prayer as a life line of communication. When we exalt the Lord with our praises, we are telling the enemy that nothing is more important than the Jesus. We cannot persevere without prayer and praise. The devil knows this. It is why he works so hard to keep you from doing it.

Read 2 Chronicles 20:21-23; 32:20-22 and Acts 16:25-34.

How important is having a personal time of prayer and praise to you?

How does the enemy try to hinder your prayer and praise time?

Notice that Paul was "maintaining His purpose." Even in the worst of circumstances he was preaching the gospel to the jailer and his house.

4. PEOPLE

The Lord has given us each other. We are the body of Christ. The Bible tells us just as our physical body is connected and registers pain, one part of Christ's church cannot hurt without the whole body being aware.

Read the passages below and think about a time when someone stood "shoulder to shoulder" with you as you persevered. Describe how that felt to know someone was praying, loving and supporting you.

Zephaniah 3:9, 2 Corinthians 1:3-5, 2 Corinthians 13:11, Romans 15:1-5

SIMPLIFY: Personal Application

As for the women who were at the cross, we don't know much of their stories after Calvary but we do know they were forever changed by their experience. We know from Scripture that some of them went to the garden tomb and were the first to know of the resurrection. It is likely that some were at the ascension and in the upper room at Pentecost. They showed up for Jesus and each other and the world would never be the same. History may never record our trials and tribulations, but heaven will. Someday Jesus will talk to each of us about how well pleased He was when we did not give up although we struggled, hurt, and grew weary. The writer of Hebrews says in verse 34 of chapter 10, *"You need to persevere so that when you have done the will of God, you will receive what he has promised."* Heaven will be full of rewards for the things we endured on earth. We must keep that perspective as we face hardships. Today we have to work. Today we have to stand. Today we have to trust. But one day we see that our "light affliction" could not compare to the glory that will be revealed (2 Corinthians 4:17).

Look back at the list of essentials and see where you might be lacking. Do you call on others for counsel? How is your prayer and praise life? Are you spending time in the Word and in the Presence of God daily?

What is one thing you can do to encourage yourself or another woman not to give up when things get hard?

SUPPLICATION: Prayer Focus

Heavenly Father, I am so thankful that you are my present help in time of trouble. I trust that when I cry out for help, you hear me. Help me to remember that this life only tells half the story. Help me to focus on my purpose and maintain my course. I know you are for me so who can be against me? When my perspective begins to change, remind me Holy Spirit that I am walking out a story written for me before I was formed in my mother's womb. Nothing that I go through catches You off guard Father. Help me remember in the darkest moments, when I feel I can't go on, that I am empowered, encouraged and equipped in Christ. In Jesus Name, Amen.

"But as for you, be strong and do not give up, for your work will be rewarded."
2 Chronicles 15:7

STORY BOARD: Journal Notes

What was revealed to you about the Character of God through HER STORY?

_____

_____

_____

_____

_____

_____

_____

_____

_____

Chosen

FOR SPIRITUAL
MOTHERING!

HER STORY

The Isaiah 54 Mother

By Melissa Patillo

"'Shout for joy, O barren one, she who has not given birth; Break forth into joyful shouting and rejoice, she who has not gone into labor [with child]! For the [spiritual] sons of the desolate one will be more numerous than the sons of the married woman,' says the Lord. 'Enlarge the site of your tent [to make room for more children]; Stretch out the curtains of your dwellings, do not spare them; Lengthen your tent ropes and make your pegs (stakes) firm [in the ground]. For you will spread out to the right and to the left; And your descendants will take possession of nations and will inhabit deserted cities.'"

ISAIAH 54:1-3b (AMP)

T he Isaiah Fifty-Four Mother is my story. I had an advanced disorder in my body and was unable to have children. This disorder led to a hysterectomy, which was the final blow. During my recovery, my dad was sitting with me and began to quote Isaiah fifty-four. The Lord began to stir my heart. My inner healing began right then and there. I had many emotions and matters of the heart to work through, but this scripture sustained me. It caused me to know that my purpose was going to be different in life. I made the decision that I was going to trust God and yield to His plan.

Even though, contextually, the Isaiah Fifty-Four Mother is addressing ancient Israel, the pain of her barrenness can be felt by any woman who has, or has had, an empty womb. But the good news is when God steps in barrenness becomes fruitfulness!

One assignment that God has given all women, whether they are natural mothers or not, is to produce spiritual children.

For many women who have never given birth to children in the natural, there is an overwhelming emptiness that only God can fill. For others who are able to give birth, there is an overwhelming joy that is beyond compare! However, one assignment that God has given all women, whether they are natural mothers or not, is to produce spiritual children. In other words, spiritually mature women need to birth/mentor younger women in the faith! If we have not partnered with God in this area, our prayer should be like that of Rachel to Jacob, *"...give me children or else I die"* (*Genesis 30:1 NKJV*).

By extracting spiritual principles from the Isaiah Fifty-Four Mother, we can see God has designed for His family to grow.

THE PURPOSE OF SPIRITUAL MOTHERHOOD
First, we see that God's purpose was for her to have many children (*Isaiah 54:1, 2*). God designed women to be nurturers. In the natural, women nurture their children. They support, encourage, train, and equip them for the future. It is no different with spiritual motherhood/mentoring. God uses spiritually mature women in unique ways to nurture, support, encourage, train, and equip the younger women in the faith (*Titus 2*). This approach not only impacts the future of the younger women, but also the generations that follow them as they continue the cycle of spiritual motherhood. This is a beautiful design of how God perpetuates His purposes in the earth and grows His kingdom.

THE FRUITFULNESS OF SPIRITUAL MOTHERHOOD

The second principle we see from our text is fruitfulness is a work of God. The barren woman could not produce children on her own. *"Shout for joy, O barren one, she who has not given birth….For the [spiritual] sons of the desolate one will be more numerous than the sons of the married woman…"* Spiritual motherhood/mentorship is an amazing process that God orchestrates as we yield our lives to Him (*Philippians 2:13*). *We teach what we know but we reproduce what we are.* Therefore, it is vital that we continue to grow spiritually and allow the Holy Spirit to develop His fruit in us (*Galatians 5:22, 23; Ephesians 5:9*). As we continuously yield to the promptings of the Holy Spirit, spiritual motherhood/mentorship will happen organically from the outflow of our own love and service to God.

THE LEGACY OF SPIRITUAL MOTHERHOOD

The third principle we see from verse three of our text is God can cause our spiritual motherhood/mentoring to impact nations. *"For you will spread out to the right and to the left; And your descendants will take possession of nations…"* We may never know the extent of our impact until we get to heaven. As we nurture, disciple, and train others we may just be training the next Deborah, Esther, or Mary! These women impacted nations and generations to the point that we are still gleaning from their lives in the 21st century!

Since my surgery, "spiritual motherhood/mentoring" has been an assignment that has brought more joy to my life than I ever imagined. God has connected me with younger people to nurture. In particular, He gave me a son, Dr. Joshua Pennington, and a daughter, Rev. Ashley Sharp. My husband and I have not only been spiritual mentors to them, but they have become such a big part of our family that they call us mom and dad and consider our house their home. They are marked by God, and both are having tremendous generational impact. It is something only God could have done. The beautiful thing is they are not the only ones that God has caused to come my way to nurture. There are many others, and only eternity will reveal the fruit that has come from my barrenness. God has a way of turning barrenness into fruitfulness!

Just like the Isaiah Fifty-Four Mother, we must all prepare for a multi-ethnic, multi-generational impact of fruitfulness!

LIFE LESSONS:

1. **THE PURPOSE OF SPIRITUAL MOTHERHOOD**: Just as ancient Israel needed "children" to survive and thrive as a nation, the Kingdom of God needs spiritual children. We not only want to empty hell and fill heaven, but we want to produce spiritual giants along the way! Spiritual motherhood/ mentoring is more needful today than at any other time in history. Society has declared an all-out war on biblical masculinity and femininity. Hyper-secular feminism has chipped away the uniqueness that women alone have. They have talked her into murdering the fruit of her womb. They have tried to tell her she is incompetent at rearing her children by allowing children to make decisions without her consent. Our young women need to be taught Godly principles to guide their lives. They need biblical perspectives on issues they face. They need to understand the pitfalls that the enemy has laid in their path to destroy them. They need to understand that there is a place they can go to gain strength for the journey and find answers to the questions of life. Where are they going to find these things? It is God's plan that they be mentored by mature women of God (*Titus 2*).

2. **THE FRUITFULNESS OF SPIRITUAL MOTHERHOOD**: God is the one who causes fruitfulness in any area of our lives. He will cause the fruit of spiritual growth and spiritual children to be abundant in our lives, but we must do our part! As we grow and mature, God will send spiritual children our way in order to glean from what we have already learned! We must have a spiritual growth plan for our own lives! This can include reading the Bible through every year (*reading in a different translation every year is always fun*), devotional studies, books, small groups, prayer, intercession, and fasting. There are many ways to grow spiritually! Our spiritual sons and daughters need us to have a plan!

3. **THE LEGACY OF SPIRITUAL MOTHERHOOD**: Ladies, let us do what the text says, *enlarge our tents, stretch out our curtains, lengthen our cords and strengthen our stakes!* Let us prepare ourselves and make room for those who God will send our way. The Kingdom of God is *multi-generational, multi-ethnic*, and *multi-cultural*. It is important that we love all *equally* and not think of any *generation*, *ethnicity*, or *culture* as less than. Jesus commissioned us to go into *all* the world and make disciples (Matthew 28:18-20). His plan is that all will come to *know* Him and *grow in* Him. I pray that He sends them from every tribe, every tongue, and every nation to us! I pray on that great

day when we stand before Him, that we will have precious fruit to lay at His feet.

YOUR STORY: Personal Reflection

She was a small, poorly educated, working class woman who dreamed of being a missionary. Gladys Aylward met no one's expectations as a world-changer, but as the scriptures tell us,

"People look at the outward appearance, but the LORD looks at the heart."
1 Samuel 16:7 NIV.

With grit and determination, she saved for years, crossed continents, and tangled with Russian police only to land in pre-World War 2 China to run a local inn. Not exactly fulfilling missionary work. As this small woman yielded her life to the service of her Lord, He blessed her in a way she could have never imagined. Gladys was chosen by God to walk as a spiritual mother to countless children! She began taking orphans in and teaching them the gospel while meeting physical needs. The Japanese attacked her province in 1938. Gladys led 100 of her children over perilous terrain to safety. Chosen Woman, you have been designed to impact others through mothering. It may not look like what you had hoped, but it will be exactly what God has planned!

How do you see God preparing you right now for spiritual motherhood/ mentoring? What does your preparation look like? Preparation time is never wasted time!

Give some examples that you have seen of generational impact through spiritual motherhood/mentoring?

Are you willing to invest the time to be a spiritual mother/mentor? It is not always convenient. It is a lot of work, prayer, and time. But it is so worth it!

Are you sensitive to the Holy Spirit enough to realize when God is bringing you spiritual children?

Are you seeing your spiritual children/mentees "reproducing" and raising disciples of Jesus? If so, how?

What are some practical ideas on how a natural mother can carve out time to also be a spiritual mother?

HIS STORY: Digging Deeper

SCRIPTURE REFERENCE:
Isaiah 54:1-3b

SETTING:
Isaiah Fifty-Four is set during the time the Babylonian Exile was over and God was ready to bring Israel back home. Israel had laid barren for so long because her people had been carried off to Babylon as a result of God's judgment. But now the anger of the Lord had passed, and God was bringing her children in abundance!

God's design has always been for generational, kingdom impact. We must prepare ourselves to take part in His plan. We can't teach what we don't know, and we can't lead where we won't go. We must have a walk with the Lord that is worth imitating. In 1 Corinthians 11:1 (TPT) Paul states, **"I want you to pattern** *your lives after me, just as I pattern mine after Chris*t." Spiritual motherhood/mentoring requires maturity on our part. We must walk, talk, and live as mature women of God. Let's dig deeper!

Re-read Isaiah 54:2-3a.

> *"Enlarge the site of your tent (to make room for more children);*
> *Stretch out the curtains of your dwellings, do not spare them;*
> *Lengthen your tent ropes and make your pegs (stakes) firm (in the*
> *ground. For you will spread out to the right and to the left;"*

What does this Scripture look like practically for us today?

Growing in our own spiritual maturity and relationship with God is an imperative part of our faith walk with God. If you don't currently have a *Spiritual Growth Plan*, or you have never really thought about creating one, start by asking yourself some of the following important questions:

Are you regularly practicing spiritual disciplines? It takes time and consistency to develop the habit of a disciplined life.

Rate yourself below on how frequently you participate in each discipline. (1=Never and 5=Always)

- Reading and Studying the Word   1 2 3 4 5
- Quiet Time with God   1 2 3 4 5
- Prayer   1 2 3 4 5
- Worship   1 2 3 4 5
- Fasting   1 2 3 4 5
- Fellowship   1 2 3 4 5

What areas do you need to develop?

NOTE: For more information on Spiritual disciplines, you may want to consider reading the transformational book *"Celebration of Discipline"* by Richard J. Foster.

Are you currently involved in ministry? *(This does not mean that you are necessarily paid staff, or even a lead teacher at the church, but are you blooming where you are planted? Are you serving and sharing your gifts, talents, and abilities?)*

How does your life influence the people around you?

Before you answer that, take a moment to recall the influence that the following CHOSEN women of the Word had on those around them:

- **What generational impact did Naomi have upon Ruth** (See: *Book of Ruth/ Her Story: Chosen,* Chapter 2)?

- **What was Deborah's influence on Barak** (See: *Judges 4, 5/Her Story: Chosen,* Chapter 11)?

- **How did Priscilla provide spiritual motherhood to Apollos** *(*See: *Acts 18:24-26/Her Story: Chosen,* Chapter 10)?

The purpose of this study is not to *compare* and *contrast* our lives with those of the women of Scripture. Their stories are meant to *inspire* us and *reveal* what God can do through the lives of women who are chosen to do His great works. Women like me and you!

How does your life influence the people around you? (Is it good, or could it be better? Do your daily attitudes and actions reflect the heart of God?)

Read Titus 2:3-5.

God never asks us to do something without telling us *how* to do it.

What does this passage teach us about spiritual motherhood/mentoring in the following areas? Fill in your answers below.

CONCEPT	SOLUTION
Biblical Marriage vs. Worldview Marriage?	
Biblical Parenting vs. Worldview Parenting?	
Biblical Home Where God is Honored vs. Worldview Home?	
What does mature Christian character look like?	
Why is self-control important?	
Why is purity important?	

Read Psalm 71:18; 78:4; 145:4.

What does the Bible say about generational impact? How should we participate in generational impact according to these passages?

Practical Considerations
for Spiritual Motherhood & Mentoring:

Intentional Listening (*James 1:19*)

- *Careful* listening is never wasted time but a powerful mentoring tool. It builds trust and causes the mentee to feel accepted, valued, and understood. This also helps them feel heard and loved!

Intentional Conversation (*Proverbs 25:11*)

- Allow God to guide conversations. Intentional listening brings about intentional conversation which can lead to transformational thinking on their part.

- Life presents daily opportunities to apply the principles of Scripture to our lives. We need to know the Word of God well enough to apply it in our daily conversations.

Intentional Discipleship (*2 Timothy 2:15*)

- Help them develop a *daily Bible reading plan* as well as other resources to help them grow.

- Take them deeper in the Word by meeting for a Bible Study. This can be done at a quaint coffee shop, a weekend getaway, or in your own home!

For book recommendations on mentoring and spiritual disciplines see appendix: Leaders Notes page 214

When we spiritually mother/mentor others, it must be done in the healthiest way possible. If not, we will be creating more problems than we are solving. There are pitfalls to watch for in this process. Consider the following:

The Pitfall of Neglected Communication (*Romans 12:10*)

- It is inconsiderate to avoid calls, texts, or other forms of communication. This teaches those who God has called you to serve that they are not valued.

- Communicate. Even if it is, *I can't talk or text right now, but I will contact you at a specific time*. Make a note if you must but do what you say you will do. This shows integrity, consideration and caring.

The Pitfall of Insensitivity (*Galatians 6:1*)

- In consideration of the time in which we live, we will have conversations that may be uncomfortable. Life can be messy. We must show great grace and sensitivity to the messiness of life when people share their lives with us.

- True healing can only take place when one can be honest and transparent without the sense of shame or disgust.

The Pitfall of Distrust (*Proverbs 16:28*)

- If people cannot trust us, they will never be able to grow and mature under us. Trust is the solid ground for all relationships. We must be trustworthy.

- Do not gossip. Breaking a confidence can destroy a relationship. Be a safe place!

The Pitfall of Neglected Priorities (*1Timothy 3:5*)

- We simply cannot neglect our own household, our husband and children, by trying to help someone else.

- We must communicate boundaries when mentoring *EGR* (*Extra Grace Required*) *persons*.

> **"Tell me and I forget, teach me and I may remember, involve me and I learn."**
>
> - Benjamin Franklin

His story will continue from generation to generation. It's exciting to be woven into the tapestry of His design for the ages. I want to *be all I can be* and *do all I can do* for Him so I will hear the commendation on that great day, *"Well done, thou good and faithful servant."* I know you do too! May we be ever fruitful!

SIMPLIFY: Personal Application

The Spirit of God beckons us through Isaiah fifty-four verse one to *"Shout for Joy"* in faith for the coming fruitfulness of our lives. We must prepare ourselves to adequately and accurately mother/mentor others. When we do, the impact we make has the capability of reaching nations and generations with His story for His glory.

What is your Spiritual Growth Plan? Can you list your Spiritual Life and Mentoring Goals?

SUPPLICATION: Prayer Focus

Father, we come to You in the name of Jesus through the power of the Holy Spirit. We thank You for turning our barrenness into fruitfulness! Help us to adequately prepare ourselves to be the spiritual mothers/mentors you want us to be. I pray that we are sensitive to what the Holy Spirit is doing in us and around us at all times. Out of the overflow of grace in our lives, may we impact many sons and daughters from every generation and every culture with Your story for Your glory. In the name of Jesus we pray.
Amen.

STORY BOARD: Journal Notes

What was revealed to you about the Character of God through HER STORY?

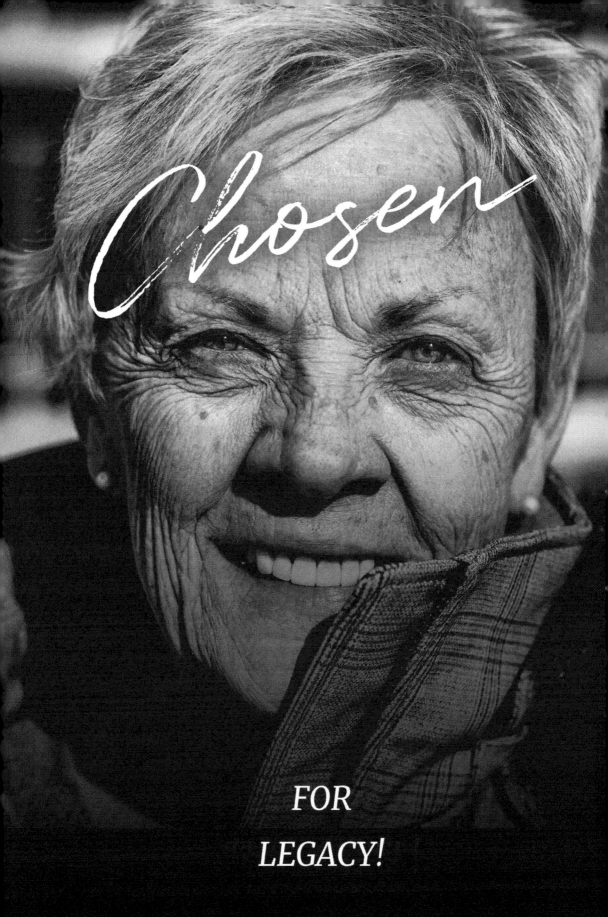

Chosen

FOR

LEGACY!

HER STORY

Lois & Eunice

By Stephanie Wheeler

"I'm reminded of how sincere your faith is. That faith first lived in your grandmother Lois and your mother Eunice. I'm Convinced that it also lives in you!"

II TIMOTHY 1:5 (GWT)

I grew up in an alcohol ravaged home, my father drank and was violent when drunk. Fear, anxiety, and hurt filled my childhood home. But a quiet retreat where acceptance, safety, and kindness were shown continually was at my grandmother's home. It was a haven for my anxious heart. She always seemed to have patience and time for me. Her home was a place of peace and unconditional love. Baking together, talking together, and just being together brought much needed security and hope.

I recall rocking each of my four sons and singing "Jesus loves you this I know for the Bible tells me so." Those precious moments when I could look into their eyes and impart the love of God through song, hugs, and prayer were the most powerful moments with my sons. Now I have the privilege of sharing my faith with my grandchildren. My "sermons" are songs and embraces sprinkled with times of play and laughter. "Oma come play with me," are God's invitations for me to share His story of love and value to the next generation. Psalm 78:4 (GWT) summarizes it well…

"We will not hide them from our children. We will tell the next generation about the LORD's power and great deeds and the miraculous things He has done!"

LOVING FAMILY
Abraham Lincoln once remarked, "no one is poor who has a Godly mother." Lois and Eunice were a paradigm of how God worked in and through relationships. We see the story of a mother and a grandmother so influenced by their relationship with God that they passionately passed on their faith to a son/grandson. Only eternity will reveal the difference that was made in countless lives or be able to calculate the value of their passing on of the stories of faith and the Word to Timothy.

LIVING FAITH
The Apostle Paul later remarked in 2 Timothy 3:14-15 (GWT), *"Timothy, continue in what you learned and found to be true. You know who your teachers were. From infancy you have known the holy Scriptures."* It would seem that Lois and Eunice took to heart and practiced what the Old Testament taught: Deuteronomy 6:7 (NLT) *"You shall repeat them again and again to your children. You shall talk about them (the promises of God) when you are at home and when you are on the road and when you are going to bed and when you are rising up."* It is clear that this grandmother and mother allowed the Word of God to work in and through them.

The faith that Lois and Eunice possessed was passed on to Timothy through the daily grind of these two women living it authentically.

A Nigerian saying says, *"**You cannot give what you do not have**."* The lesson of Lois and Eunice is really quite simple. Lois believed, and the sincere faith that she possessed was passed on to her daughter Eunice who then passed it on to her son, Timothy. It was a faith lived in spite of the social/cultural dominance of a harsh Roman government and a seeming "absentee father," (whether by choice or circumstance). The faith that Lois and Eunice possessed was passed on to Timothy through the daily grind of these two women living it authentically.

More than likely they passed on their sincere faith through their *actions* and not just their *words*. Even with all of the endless daily demands that parents face: jobs, chores, meals, and raising a family, it would seem Lois was able to devote some "special" time to Timothy. This grandmother may have been the "listening ear" to Timothy's inquisitive questions while mom was busy earning a living. Through her gift of time to Timothy, Lois may have cultivated the soil of his heart preparing it for the verbal impartation of the words of faith.

LASTING LEGACY

It seems like only yesterday my husband David was driving me to the labor and delivery room at St Joseph's hospital in Minot, North Dakota for the birth of our eldest son Jeremiah. Now forty years later, in what seems like just a blink of the eye, Jeremiah and his wife Valerie just recently delivered TWINS! Through times and seasons, good or difficult, our family has clearly understood one thing—GOD IS FAITHFUL! Over the years Jesus has walked beside us. And when we couldn't walk another step, He carried us through the deepest unexpected sorrows as well as the highest undeserved blessings. His presence and Word have been our sword, shield, comfort, and guide.

I believe passing on this life of authentic faith for both Lois and Eunice was as natural to them as breathing air. The "inheritance" they passed on was embedded in God's ongoing story. Yet in the midst of "THEIR story," God unfolded "HIS story!" The presence and promises of God inspired and empowered Lois, then Eunice, and ultimately Timothy. And through the inspiration of the Holy Spirit, Timothy wrote the Scriptures that have impacted multiple generations and nations!

LIFE LESSONS:

1. **LOVING FAMILY**: Not everyone has a loving, Christian home, or family. If this, is you, don't be discouraged because God will send you mentors and leaders in this *family of faith* to help you grow! The family of God often steps in where natural families struggle. On the flip side, you may just be the Lois or Eunice to a Timothy or a young lady that needs your authentic faith! We are called to disciple others in the Body of Christ. Who is God calling you to disciple today?

2. **LIVING FAITH**: It is so important that we live out our faith authentically. The world has seen enough insincere faith. Just simply living our authentic faith, regardless of the circumstances we find ourselves in, will be an example to those around us as well as those whom God has called us to disciple. Living our authentic faith may be seen in the daily tasks of serving our families, churches, or others. It may be seen in the time we invest to speak a word in "due season (Proverbs 15:23)," or in the sweet lullaby to our grandchildren. Regardless of how it is shared, our faith must be genuine and bold!

3. **LASTING LEGACY**: Families that embrace the generations by incorporating grandparents, aunts, uncles, and extended family members create opportunities for security, "roots," and value to be passed on to their children. Through Lois a "sincere" faith was displayed and passed on to Eunice and ultimately to Timothy. You never know what generational or even multi-generational impact you will have on your family or others by simply living out your authentic faith! *"One generation shall praise Your works to another and shall declare Your mighty acts"* (Psalm 145:4). This is a lasting legacy!

YOUR STORY: Personal Application

Every one of us functions as a link in a chain. We connect to others in every way possible—friends, family, church, work, and so on. Each person occupies a place in every other life that only they can fill. You may have heard or used the expression, *"a chain is only as strong as its weakest link."* Regarding Christian legacy, every link is as strong as the next because every life represented is "in Christ." In Colossians chapter two Paul desired that we be *"knit together by strong ties of love."* It doesn't matter if you had a horrible background or the greatest life ever. At the cross, we all begin life the same—loved by Jesus and commissioned by Him to change the world. God is a God of order and systems. Just before He ascended, Jesus gave His followers the plan for impacting the world. Acts 1:8 tells us- *"...and you will be my witnesses in Jerusalem, and in all Judea and Samaria, and to the ends of the earth."* God's first step in His plan for us to change the world has been to start with those closest to us.

Family can be the primary channel for expanding the kingdom of God. A family that places an importance on passing down a faith heritage has unlimited potential for impact.

What extended family member has made the greatest positive influence in your life?

A great minister once stated, *"The Holy Spirit will not allow a void in God's kingdom."* Many, like Timothy, understand what it means to have a lack of "spiritual guidance" from a father. Perhaps you are the same.

If the above question is blank, how has the Lord filled the void for you?

If you are the one Jesus provided to fill the void for someone else, explain that experience. What did you do? How did the Lord open the door for you?

How might the Church come along side and provide for struggling young families today?

You may not realize this, but God has designed you to fit perfectly into His body. Your gifts, calling, talents, personality bent and even food preferences all work together to equip you to leave a legacy.

Fill out the box below. Think of anything you like to do or feel called to do. Then think of any person or group of people who could be blessed by your love in action. (For example, "cooking" could impact a sick or elderly person. If you know a specific person by name, list them.)

What I Can Do	Who I Can Impact

Never say you can't make a difference. Chosen woman you are designed to make a difference! Stick with God's plan and reach the ones closest to you. You might be surprised at the result.

Many of our Bible heroines have entire chapters or even entire books written for our benefit and edification. Consider Ruth, Esther, and Deborah. But for Lois and Eunice there is only one direct reference found about their story in the entire Bible. The Apostle Paul, when writing to his protégé Timothy, said these words: "I'm reminded of how sincere your faith is. THAT FAITH first lived in your grandmother Lois and your mother Eunice. I'm convinced that it also lives in you!" (2 Timothy 1:5 GWT) Only one verse but that verse is packed with life and encouragement! Dear one if you feel your story doesn't make headline news, or your story is rather mundane, take heart! The one verse dedicated to Lois and Eunice explodes with the life and the promises of God.

Read John 15:5

What did Jesus say would happen if we remain in Him?

What does remaining in Him look like in your life?

He knows YOUR name!

Often in Scripture the name a person was given held significance. Look up the following names and match their meaning: (Note: most are found in the chapters of this Bible study book.)

RUTH   ____   a. resembling a bee; a prophetess

DEBORAH ____   b. a star: a Queen who saved her nation

ESTHER   ____   c. superior; the grandmother of Timothy

EUNICE   ____   d. companion/friend; great grandmother of David

LOIS   ____   e. good victory; mother of Timothy

Now note how each of those women were chosen by God in His plans. Look up the meaning of your name for fun. You may see God's design behind it.

Your Name _____

Meaning _____

God knows your name. He has a purpose and a plan for you. You are not here by accident nor are you just passing through.

"You are *Chosen* by God with a
high calling and a unique mission."
- Stephanie Wheeler

HIS STORY: Digging Deeper

SCRIPTURE REFERENCES: Read Her Story!
II Timothy 1:5, 3:14-15; Acts 16:1

SIGNATURE:
LOIS (LOE-iss: "better; companion/friend"- Grandmother of Timothy).
EUNICE (YOO-niss: "good victory"- Mother of Timothy).

SETTING:
[Date: Around A.D. 30.] God's people often find themselves in "perilous times." Lois and Eunice were no exception. The crushing hand of Roman oppression was the daily lot of Lois and Eunice. Though some "freedom" was extended to the subjugated nation of Israel, for the most part, nothing was done in Judea without the glaring eye of "Big Brother" constantly watching and dictating what actions were acceptable and what actions were not. *But God's promises are never bound!*

Mother Theresa said, "If you want to change the world, go home and love your family." Well, not exactly. My apologies if you have this on a plaque in your home, it's still a great thought. Her original quote has been paraphrased into a pithy tweet. It's catchy, it's concise, and we love it but the actual statement she made carries much more gravitas. The following is an excerpt from her 1984 Nobel Peace Prize acceptance speech. Consider her words:

> "And so, my prayer for you is that truth will bring prayer in our homes, and the fruit of prayer will be that we believe that in the poor, it is Christ. And if we will really believe, we will begin to love. And if we love, naturally, we will try to do something. First in our own home, our next door neighbor, in the country we live, in the whole world."

She understood that developing a legacy was equal to making an impact. Anyone, anywhere, can make that happen. We must understand that Jesus has chosen each of us to cultivate legacy in our relationships. Legacy is developed by living a life of authentic faith. We must be like Eunice and Lois as stated previously: "I believe passing on this life of authentic faith for both Lois and Eunice was as natural to them as breathing air." It did not become a part of them, they became a part of it through transformation. A life of authentic faith is produced by spending time in God's presence and a commitment to obey His Word. You cannot pass on what you do not possess.

Read Deuteronomy 11:1-21

Deuteronomy is one of those books that we hurry through in our yearly reading. It is a "second law" or retelling of the law that God dictated to Moses. If you have skimmed the book of Deuteronomy, you are not alone. However, the book of Deuteronomy is very important. When the Bible refers to "the law of the Lord," it is referencing Deuteronomy. It is the book that inspired King Josiah's reforms. Ezra read from Deuteronomy at the Festival of Booths. It is considered the "heart of the Torah," and it is one of the top three books that our Lord quoted during His earthly ministry. With this in mind, please re-read the passage.

What is the message of Deuteronomy 11:1-21?

Verse 8 begins a discourse on the Blessings of Obedience- those blessings are contingent upon what?

In verses 18-20 the reader is instructed to incorporate the Word into his/her daily life. What are those specific instructions?

1.

2.

3.

4.

5.

6.

7.

8.

Jewish families had an object called a *mezuzah*, a parchment bearing the Word of the Lord. The Mezuzah had two functions, because It was also a case or container that held the parchment.

- Whenever a Jew would enter or leave home, the Mezuzah reminded them of their covenant with God.
- The Mezuzah was a symbol to everyone who came by the home that it was a place where the Law of the Lord was held in high regard and obeyed.

Legacy begins with incorporating the Word of God into your home.

What ways (other than beautiful religious plaques and décor) have you incorporated God's Word into your home?

How do you live according to Deuteronomy 11:18-20?

In the previous chapter, Moses recounts when the Lord instructed him to remake the stone tablets containing the law. Remember, Moses smashed the first ones, but God gave Moses another opportunity to get the Word to His people. God wants you to know His Word, He isn't hiding anything from you. He knows if you understand the Word and obey it, you will teach it to your family or those whom you influence. You teach with your words, actions, and reactions. As the Word impacts you, it will impact those around you, legacy will be passed, and part of your purpose will be satisfied. Most importantly GOD WILL GET THE GLORY!

The Word of God has the power to transform lives. Transformed lives impact their worlds and create legacies of faith. The Word MUST be a priority in every home. Timothy learned this from his grandmother and mother.

Who is learning the Word from you?
Look up the following Scriptures and fill in the blanks:

- **Hebrews 4:12 KJV** *"For the Word of God is _____ and _____ and is _____ than any _____ sword."*

- **I Peter 1:25 NKJV** *"The Word of the Lord endures _____."*

- **Isaiah 40:8 KJV** *"The grass _____, the flower _____ but the Word of our God shall _____ forever."*

- **Colossians 3:16 KJV** *"Let the Word of Christ dwell in you _____ in all wisdom; _____ and admonishing one another in _____ and _____, and spiritual _____."*

- **Jeremiah 20:9 KJV** *"......But his _____ was in mine heart as a burning _____ shut up in my bones"*

He has given YOU His Word!

Reflect on the meaning behind the Scriptures above. How powerful and important is the Word of God in your life? Share your thoughts?

Read Joshua 4

This chapter is about remembering. Israel was finally receiving their promise we read from Deuteronomy. The Lord warned them to not forget it was He who brought them through. He wanted them to pass on the account of His faithfulness on to their children.

Where were they to get the stones for the memorial? What was the significance of getting the stones from that place?

How were they to answer their children when they asked about the stones?

What does the last verse of this chapter have to do with legacy?

Time passes quickly, it is important to make the most of it. Legacy is born, built and passed on in this life.

Lois and Eunice practiced their faith by incorporating the directives found in Scripture and passing them down.

We often think the legacy we leave must be something huge, grand or earthshaking. Surely the more grand people are impacted the more God is pleased. Not so. In God's kingdom, the simple gestures are often the ones that speak volumes to the next generation. Jesus gave us a simple directive, "Remember Me." When you participate in the celebration of communion, you preach an illustrated sermon of the gospel of Jesus.

Read Luke 22:14-21
Where were Jesus and His disciples having this meal?

Fill in the box below and answer the question:
What were the elements served and what did they represent?

ELEMENTS	MEANING

Do you take communion in your home? Why or Why not?

If you were discipling another, what would you teach them regarding communion?

What age is appropriate for allowing children to participate in communion?

Read 1 Corinthians 11:26
How important is taking communion in relation to leaving a legacy of faith?

God sees the end from the beginning and can envision far more than we can imagine. Do not under estimate His ability to bless your life with influence.

Read Ephesians 3:20 (KJV). Fill in the blanks:

"Now unto to Him who is able to do _____ abundantly above

all that we _____ or _____, according to

the _____ that works in us, to Him be glory."

Whatever obstacle we may face, the **ONE** we serve, the **ONE** whose story of redemption we have become a part of, has the plans and power to do way beyond our expectations and dreams. Who knows who *He* may raise up to come along-side the "sincere faith" you are displaying and passing on.

Fun Facts: About Lois and Eunice

♦ There is only one mention of these ladies in Holy Scripture and yet what a powerful impact they had in their somewhat hidden influence.

♦ Eunice most likely raised Timothy in the town of Lystra, a Roman colony with no synagogue. Today the town exists as Klistra, Turkey.

♦ Eunice and Lois mentored young Timothy not realizing that he later would become the Pastor at the Ephesus church.

♦ Eunice was married to a Greek man. He was not of like faith. Yet this did not hinder the fact that she had been chosen for legacy.

♦ According to biblical tradition Lois was born into a Jewish faith and later became a Christ follower with her daughter Eunice.

SIMPLIFY: Personal Application

Lois and Eunice stand as a reminder of the power of a "***sincere faith***." What they possessed was passed on through simple deeds and actions of mercy and grace. The "*obstacles*" they faced were no match for the powerful Word they possessed. Though only *one verse* in the Bible is dedicated to them, it speaks volumes to us.

Today take inventory of what God has bestowed in you. Be specific as you identify your God given interests and abilities. Pray to the Lord of the Harvest to reveal those whom you might share your "***sincere faith.***" Is there a young mom or single dad who could really benefit from your time and nurturing?

Now give those gifts, talents and abilities to God and ask Him to direct you to the individual(s) whom He desires. You are a channel of God's love and Word to the next generation. YOU GO GIRL!

SUPPLICATION: Prayer Focus

Lord, *"the story goes on,"* so here I am. You created me uniquely for Your purposes and Glory. I give myself to You whole heartedly and unreservedly. May the power of Your Word and Spirit dwell in me and work through me. Guide me to those you have prepared that I may be a blessing to them as well as my children and grandchildren, and future generations.

In Jesus name, Amen.

STORY BOARD: Journal Notes

What was revealed to you about the Character of God through HER STORY?

Chosen with a Purpose

JOHN 15:16

Chosen

FOR

BREAKTHROUGH!

HER STORY

Hannah

By Andrea Dunn

"So, Hannah rose up after they had eaten in Shiloh, and after they had drunk. Now Eli the priest sat upon a seat by a post of the temple of the Lord. And she was in bitterness of soul, and prayed unto the Lord, and wept sore."

1 SAMUEL 9-10 (KJV)

Have you ever yearned for something so badly that it consumed every moment of the day? Like Hannah, I have been at a place in my Christian life where the feeling of rejection and abandonment preoccupied my thoughts. It was only when I allowed myself to be consumed with the words and presence of God that I was able to find a sense of relief.

Hannah was a woman chosen by God to give birth to one of the greatest prophets of all time. She was the wife of a prominent man. She was deeply loved by her husband, but she had a major obstacle, she was barren. Although chosen, God shut up her womb (1 Samuel 1:5). God closing her womb seems unimaginable, but as the story unfolds we see God was orchestrating the events of her life. He had a plan!

Hannah was identified as the barren woman, but she failed to identify herself as others saw her.

Due to Hannah's barrenness, she constantly felt humiliated and ashamed. It was all because of the taunting of her adversary, Peninnah (*Elkahana's other wife*). Hannah was identified as *the barren woman*, but she failed to identify herself as others saw her. Instead, she chose to stay in the presence of God where she was able to get affirmation of her identity in Him.

Although in a state of anguish, Hannah stayed in the presence of God and interceded for a son. In observation of Hannah's life, we see that she came to the place where she decided to pursue her breakthrough. Her desire for a breakthrough was the catalyst for her one-on-one relationship with God that brought forth her miracle. She didn't want to be identified as *the barren wife of Elkanah*. It was a time for a change! It was time for a breakthrough! It was time to intercede!

You are so close to your breakthrough, hang in there! Don't lose hope now!

PERSPECTIVE BEFORE THE BREAKTHROUGH
Hannah's perspective before her breakthrough was important. She was sad, broken, had stopped eating, and was constantly weeping. Her adversary made things even more difficult for her. The teasing and taunting further exacerbated her feeling of brokenness. The culture marked her by her barrenness, and her future was in jeopardy as to her care in the winter season of life. However, the source of her identity was not found in what was happening *around* her. The source of her identity was found in what was *within* her.

Our perspective before the breakthrough is important. Pain is nothing more than an indicator that something is wrong. Our pain is not who we are! We may *experience a season* of lack, barrenness, persecution, or anxiety but seasons do not define us! We must let what is *IN* us be greater than what is *AROUND* us!

Hannah turned to the one thing she knew best! It was the very thing that would counteract the plan of the enemy—Prayer! She was provoked into a season of prayer. *Do you have a need that is driving you into a season of prayer?* It's

Important that you don't let the season define you! Find your chosen identity and breakthrough on your knees!

PRAYER FOR THE BREAKTHROUGH

Hannah's story provides us with examples of how we, as daughters of God, can go before our Father when we are in pain. She found herself at a place where she pursued prayer passionately and persistently.

The Bible says we should pray *without ceasing* (1 Thessalonians 5:17). That is praying *in every season*. James 5:16 (KJV) states, *"...the effectual fervent prayer of a righteous man availeth much."* *"Effectual fervent"* in the Greek means *very strong*. It could be rendered *literally, "very strong is the supplication of a righteous man, energizing."* Oh, how we need to pray with fervency and effectiveness! When we put energy into our prayer, the effectiveness will be very strong!

One song writer wrote in regard to prayer, "Sweet hour of prayer, sweet hour of prayer that draws me from a world of care." Oh, for the sweet hour of prayer that in seasons of distress and grief our soul will often find relief! Our prayers can have a powerful impact on any situation we face.

PRAISE FOR THE BREAKTHROUGH

Prayer is a powerful tool that God wants us to use to stay connected with Him, strengthen our inner man, and use as a weapon to overcome the tactics of the enemy. It may appear that victory is not any time soon, but we are not moved by what we see, hear, or feel. We are women of faith! Our identity is not in what happens around us, but it is found in Jesus Christ! When troublesome times come, God desires for us to draw closer to Him. We will be victorious through Christ Jesus!

"But thanks be to God, which giveth us the victory through our Lord Jesus Christ."
1 Corinthians 15:57 (KJV)

Hannah turned to the one thing she knew best, It was the very thing that would counteract the plan of the enemy— PRAYER!

LIFE LESSON:

1. **PERSPECTIVE.** While being teased and taunted by others, labeled by society, or slapped in the face every morning by the lies of the enemy when we look in the mirror, we have a choice! You can choose to not believe the lies or sink in the pain! You can choose to look up to the Truth! Begin to focus on who the Bible says you are! You are not defined by others! You are not defined by your circumstance! You are defined by your Heavenly Father! You are defined as a CHOSEN DAUGHTER OF GOD!

2. **PRAYER.** In the midst of your own deep pain, you can call out to God and find peace. It is through your prayer and intercession that you develop a closer relationship with God which provides strength and comfort for another day. No prayer, no power. Much prayer, much power!

3. **PRAISE.** Victory may seem years away, but know this—you are a *victor*, not a *victim*! Don't be moved by your senses but by the Word of God that let's you know you already possess the victory because of *whose* you are! Because of this truth you can praise God in the midst of praying for your breakthrough!

YOUR STORY: Personal Application

When the realization that you have been chosen to believe for a breakthrough comes into focus, the first and only response must be faith.

> *"And without faith it is impossible to please Him, for whoever*
> *would draw near to God must believe that He exists and*
> *that He rewards those who seek Him"*
> Hebrews 11:6 (ESV).

Chosen Woman, as you stand at the threshold of your breakthrough, your thoughts and petitions must be bathed in prayer and faith. You can be certain the enemy will use this time to try and hinder both of those efforts.

Consider Hannah.

Why do you think God had shut up Hannah's womb?

Have you ever been in the place where the Lord shut doors to your natural abilities to show His power in your life? Explain.

How might we follow Hannah's example when we struggle with the schemes the enemy brings while we wait?

Have you ever yearned for something so badly that it consumed your every moment of the day? Have you ever thought enough is enough? Are you ready for a season of change? Keep your hope in the Lord! He holds your days and seasons! He has perfect timing for His plans for you!

Read Romans 4:18 and Hebrews 6:19.

This flower represents you believing for your breakthrough. The center is your heart full of hope in the Lord. The petals represent your prayers. The hope in your heart sustains you in the waiting. Hope gives life to our needs like the heart of a flower feeds the petals that make up its beauty.

Write your prayers on or around the petals.

Think of the center of the flower as your heart filled with hope.

Sometimes the breakthroughs we need come immediately. Sometimes they are found in seasons of waiting.

Read Proverbs 13:12.
Can you see how crucial it is to fill your heart with hope in the Lord?

How might you, like Hanna, maintain a hopeful heart in order to keep your prayer effective?

HIS STORY: Digging Deeper

SCRIPTURE REFERENCES: Read Her Story!
1 Samuel 1:1-36, 1 Samuel 2:1-10

SIGNATURE:
HANNAH [HAN-nuh: "grace and favor"]—Mother of Samuel, Israel's last judge.

SETTING:
[About 1125 B.C.] In ancient Israel, children were considered a sign of God's blessing (Psalm 127:3). The ability to bear children in Hannah's time and culture was a matter of significance. Hannah was barren and unable to conceive a child for a long time after marrying. This brought about disgrace and humiliation for her. Hannah's infertility coin-cided with a time of spiritual barrenness and natural drought, and lack. God's people were involved in every sinful act imaginable and there was a lack of Godly leaders. However, Hannah and her family went to the temple to pray year after year. God had a plan for her.

Fun Facts: About Hannah

- The name Hannah means "Favor or Grace"
- Hannah is the fourth woman in the Bible to experience infertility, (Sarah, Rebekah and Rachel were before her) yet her response is different than the others. When Eli the priest told her she would conceive, her countenance changed, and she believed the Word of the Lord
- The blessing did not stop with her son Samuel. Eli prophesied over her, and she had 5 more children.
- Hannah's husband had two wives.

Q & A: Why did her husband have two wives?

"Polygamy (two wives) was a fact of life in the ancient world. However, the Bible never puts polygamy in a favorable light. Strife and conflict always characterize polygamous families in the Bible."
-David Guzik

When God is preparing us to receive, you can be certain that He is working in areas other than your most pressing need. He knows when, where and how to bring about growth. Trust Him. He stepped into your life at the perfect moment, brought you into His family, and now He will walk you through this wonderful story He has written just for you! **Don't miss the breakthroughs that come disguised as God's goodness.** Recognizing these in your life will prove to be stones you will stand on when you wait for the Lord to move in the more apparent ones.

Eli the priest didn't know what was going on with Hannah, neither did her husband. People around you may not understand what is going on inside of you. They may think they know; they may even act as if they know. But only God, your Heavenly Father knows what's in your heart. **God heard Hannah's cry and he answered in His own time.**

Read Galatians 4:4

What does this verse tell you about God's timing for your life?

Read Ephesians 1:4

What does this verse tell you about God's plans for your life?

You have heard the expression, *"When you're down to nothing, God is up to something?"* When we come to know Hannah in 1 Samuel chapter 1 she is a miserable shell of a once-hopeful young bride. The years and Peninnah have not been kind. Hanna is physically, emotionally, and spiritually bankrupt. She is empty in every way. She is not alone. As Naomi arrived in Bethlehem, she declared **"I went out full, but the Lord has brought me back empty."** The word of God tells story after story of men and women who found themselves in challenging times. With resources depleted and options exhausted, they were ripe for destruction. We are no different. Seasons of loss, pain, and suffering plague us all. We try to carry on but often find ourselves staring into a bleak future. God's desire for us is to trust Him even in EVERY situation. The empty vessel held by its Creator is in the best position to overflow with the miraculous.

WIDOW AT ZAREPHATH-

God moves for women who are out of options.

Read 1 Kings 17:8-16

Answer the following True or False Questions:

        T / F   The Lord sent Elijah to a widow in Israel.

        T / F   The widow and her son were gathering sticks for a fire.

        T / F   Elijah helped her gather the sticks.

        T / F   The widow was going to cook a feast

The widow tells Elijah her plans. He responds in verse 13 and 14.

What is God saying to the widow through His prophet?

How did the Lord reward the widow's obedience?

Unfortunately, receiving greatly from the Lord does not mean we grow and change. It also does not make us immune to future troubles.

Read verses 17-24 and answer the following True or False Questions:

T / F   The widow's son got married and left her alone.

T / F   The widow's son got sick and died because she was a sinner.

T / F   God gave the widow another miracle.

T / F   The widow's greatest need was for physical hunger.

Zarephath means *"smelting place."* Smelting is the process in which metals are extracted from its ore. Different processes are used on different metals. Gold, the most precious, has an extreme smelting process. It is pulverized and heated in excess of 1064 degrees Celsius. When the gold is pure, it can be formed. God brings us to "smelting places" to prepare us for our purpose.

The beauty is- while we think the goal is to receive our *breakthrough,* the Lord's purpose is to prepare us for more!

Read Job 23:10.
How comforting is it to know that God knows exactly where you are and where you are headed? What is the end goal of verse 10?

What was God's goal for the widow in 1 Kings 17:24?   What was her declaration?

Read Jeremiah 22:11
What is the only answer a believer can give to this question?

Hanna was empty of everything except her desire to cry out to the Lord. With every ounce of life left in her body she poured and poured, and poured. The petition had no "amen," there was no end to her craving, there was no end to her drive. Watchman Nee said of fervent prayer, *"Until we begin to bleed in the place of prayer, we can never be a blessing to others."* Hanna prayed to point of perceived drunkenness. Composure had no place in her entreaty. She had no idea her pursuit would yield the answer for her nation in the birth of Samuel. Likewise, we cannot comprehend the full impact of our prayers when we believe for a miracle. We know God is good. He hears us and **"God causes everything to work together for the good of those who love God and are called according to His purpose for them"** Romans 8:28 (NLT). This should create in us a custom of persistence.

Don't stop praying! Pray with fervency! Pray with passion and consistency!

PERSISTENT WIDOW—
Jesus moves for women who always pray and never give up.

Read Luke 18:1-8
God has always heard the prayers of those whose culture tried to silence. Jesus spoke of such an one in this parable on prayer. This widow was poor and power-less. Her only hope of justice was a man so evil the scriptures state, **"He neither feared God nor cared about people."** He had a reputation for ruling with no care for his fellow man. She had no option except persistence.

According to the parable, how did this widow approach the wicked judge?

How did the judge respond?

Then, in a beautiful juxtaposition, Jesus reveals the heart of the Father toward those who *"always pray and never give up."*
What is the contrast Jesus poses to His listeners in verses 6 and 7?

What is your answer to Jesus' question in verse 8?

The Word of God gives us much inspiration for persistent prayer. When we obey scripture our faith is strengthened, and our resolve solidified.

Look up the scriptures and fill out the box below. Write God's instructions and your response to those instructions. Your responses are found in your heart.

Scripture	Instruction	Response
Psalm 3:3-4		
Psalm 42:6		
Isaiah 26:3		
Matthew 7:7		
James 4:2		

PRAISE AND THANKSGIVING-
Read Psalm 34:1-3.

Hannah offered up praise and thanksgiving to God in one of the most poetic and stunning prayers ever written. Her prayer begins with praise to the Lord for what He has done. It then grows into worship for who He is. Her prayer serves as a model for us. As we pray. As we wait. Let us remember the Lord is our ONLY source and hope! He will be ever worthy of our praise and worship regardless of when or how He answers!

Read 1 Samuel 2:1-2 NIV and Fill in the blanks below:

"My heart _____ in the LORD;

My horn is _____ high.

My mouth _____ over my enemies, for

I _____ in your deliverance.

'There is no one _____ like the LORD;

There is no one _____ you;

There is no _____ like our God.'"

SIMPLIFY: Personal Application

You may be going through a season of brokenness and feel as if there is no way out. But girl, you've been chosen to believe for a breakthrough! **My challenge for you is to not only plan for it, but follow through.**

- **Put "TIME WITH GOD" on your schedule-** Find time to daily spend with Him.
- **Go to a specific quite place.** Go where you can, like Hannah, spend some alone time with God.
- **Stay focused.** Don't focus on what others are saying *to* you or *about* you. Don't focus on your situation (past or current) but focus on the One who gives the breakthrough.
- **Give Him Praise for your Breakthrough.** Believe that it is on the way! "Raise a hallelujah in the presence of your enemies!"

Let's make a plan. Fill out the following graph:

HANNAH	INSERT YOUR NAME
	_____
Hannah's NEED: Her womb was shut up. She needed a child.	My NEED/S: **What are your greatest needs?**
Hannah's GOALS: To reach out to God through intercessory prayer.	My GOAL/S: **What do you intend to do about it?**
Hannah's TASKS: She prayed consistently, passionately, sincerely, and trusted in her God for deliverance.	My TASK/S: **How will you accomplish the goal that you set?**
Hannah's PROMISE: *And she made a vow, saying, "O Lord Almighty, if you will only look upon your servant's misery and remember me, and not forget your servant but give her a son, then I will give him to the Lord for all the days of his life, and no razor will even be used on his head."* (1 Samuel 1:11)	My PROMISE: **What will you surrender to Him?**
Hannah's PRAISE: *In the LORD my horn is lifted high.* *My mouth boasts over my enemies,* *for I delight in your deliverance.* *'There is no one holy like the LORD;* *there is no one besides you;* *there is no Rock like our God.'*	MY PRAISE: **What will your praise report look like?**

SUPPLICATION: Prayer Focus

Lord, I may not understand the plans You have for me, but I do know that they were strategically arranged in order for me to fulfill my purpose. Teach me how to trust in You and wait upon You for my miracle breakthrough. I have been chosen to believe You and trust that Your timing is better than my own. I now commit myself to a closer relationship with You through persistent, breakthrough, believing prayer. You are my rock, and I will forever praise You. I give myself to You, use me for your glory, in Jesus' name.
Amen.

STORY BOARD: Journal Notes

What was revealed to you about the Character of God through HER STORY?

Chosen

FOR
BRAVERY!

HER STORY:

Jael

By Allison Smallwood

*"So, on that day God subdued Jabin the king of
Canaan before the people of Israel."*
JUDGES 4:23 (ESV)

I grew up down an old gravel road in a very small town in the middle of nowhere Missouri. My parents split up early in my life and I was raised with an abusive stepfather and five brothers. Poverty was all around and just part of the "norm" in my neck of the woods. As I approached adulthood, I could not shake this undeniable feeling that I did not belong and there had to be a greater purpose for my life. I was no different than anyone else I grew up with. There were no "special circumstances," just ordinary people in an ordinary life called to do extraordinary things! That was what I got a hold of even after years of being told, "Nothing good comes out of that town."

121

Jael doesn't normally fall on the Christians top ten list. Maybe she's overlooked because her story is pretty gruesome, taboo, and goes against so many cultural and social norms—then, and now! Nevertheless, God chose HER to be brave and bring freedom to the Israelites.

Jael's story is significant because God chose to use someone as unlikely as her to fulfill His will.

When Barak told Deborah that he needed her to accompany him to war against the Canaanites, she said something very significant. *"...I will surely go with you. Nevertheless, the road on which you are going will not lead to your glory, for the Lord will sell Sisera into the hand of a woman..." (Judges 4:9 ESV).* Can we all pause and make the "gasp" sound that is going through our heads as we read this?

THE OPPORTUNITY FOR BRAVERY
Sisera, commander of the Canaanite army, fled on foot in an effort to save his own life! This is where it starts to get spicy! Sisera comes to the camp where Jael lived. Her husband, Heber, was an ally to Canaanite King Jabin, so Sisera had no reason to fear or question her motives. They spoke and she was hospitable. Upon inviting him into her tent, he asks for water, but she gives him milk. So many questions here, right? Was milk to make him more comfortable? Maybe to lull him to sleep? We don't really know. He laid down, she covered him with a rug and then he asked her to guard the door and if anyone asks if he is there, to say "no." I have to be honest, as I read this, I can't help but think "player just got PLAYED!"

THE OPERATION OF BRAVERY
Sisera fell asleep and the Bible actually says that Jael picked up a tent peg and a hammer and went "softly" to him, driving the peg into his temple until it went INTO THE GROUND! She is *STRONG, FIERCE,* and *BRAVE*! I have a feeling that had she been "equipped" with a common weapon of battle she might have been shaky and anxious. Instead, she picked up tools that she was very skilled at using.

Sometimes there is an obedience to God that weighs heavier than any earthly relationships.

So as Barak was chasing him, Jael came out of her tent and was like, "oh hey, here's the guy you're looking for." That is how we end with the honor of killing the captain of Jabin's army going to a woman! On that day, *"God subdued Jabin, the king of Canaan, before the people of Israel."* This verse is vital in knowing what Jael did brought honor to God. She didn't have a personal vendetta against Sisera. The Word actually says that they were allies. She had no earthly reason to kill him. But sometimes there is an obedience to God that weighs heavier than any earthly relationships.

THE OVERVIEW OF BRAVERY

So now we find ourselves asking why she would have killed him? After much research we see that the Kenites were closely related to the Midianites, who at times were dwelling with the Israelites. They had to be aware of Jabin's oppression of the Israelites. What Jael did went totally against everything she should have done from every perspective! She saw an opportunity to help God's people and she went against the rules of the current culture to help the oppressed!

LIFE LESSONS:

1. **THE OPPORTUNITY FOR BRAVERY**: Sometimes the opportunities that God puts right in front of you won't make sense to you or those around you! You will have to do it, afraid! Ignore all the "what if's" and doubts in yourself and your abilities. When God is asking something of you sometimes you don't have long to respond. Often, delayed obedience is disobedience. Situations and current culture moves so fast around us. So, if it is not going to be you, He will ask someone else to step up! God's will must be done!

2. **THE OPERATION OF BRAVERY**: GIRL, USE WHAT YOU'VE GOT! In biblical times, women were in charge of setting up tents and repairing them. Jael was skilled and strong. You think the tent peg was the weapon of choice? She wasn't in the army or "in battle" but she was skilled. You may not always have access to what you think you need, in order to do what God is asking of you, but YOU ALREADY HAVE WHAT YOU NEED to get the job done! Where's the faith and trust in Him when we "feel" equipped and ready in our own skills and resources? (2 Corinthians 3:5-6)

3. **THE OVERVIEW OF BRAVERY**: Sometimes there is a deeper purpose than following all the rules. Even today this event makes Christians uncomfortable, and honestly, some may not consider her a hero. But the Bible proves differently when Deborah praises her in song in Judges 5. Who does that sound like? Jesus! Healing on the Sabbath, touching lepers even though the rule stated that he would be considered "unclean." Heavenly rules are greater than earthly religious rules.

YOUR STORY: Personal Reflection

"She showed a lot of courage. She never cried. She didn't whimper. She just marched along like a little soldier, and we're all very proud of her." Deputy Marshal Charles Burks (describing Ruby Bridges demeanor on her first day at W.F. Elementary).

Starting a new school can make a child anxious, but for six-year-old Ruby Bridges it was a life-changing experience that shifted cultural norms and made her the face of the civil rights movement in November 1960. Ruby was the first child of color to attend the newly desegregated William Frantz Elementary School in New Orleans, LA. Ruby, her mother Lucille, and four federal marshals walked past angry crowds of protestors to get into the school. A parent-led boycott meant she was the only student in attendance. All but one faculty member refused to accept Ruby as a student. She spent the first day in the principal's office because of the chaos.

The next day the boycott was broken by Rev. Lloyd A. Foreman as he walked his daughter Pam to her empty classroom. The Bridges and Foreman's paid a high price for their bravery. Her father, Abon Bridges, lost his job. Her mother, Lucille, was denied entry at the local grocery store. The Foreman's home was vandalized and threatened with explosives. When Nyra Foreman expressed concern for her daughter's safety, Pam replied, *"I'll be ok as long as I'm with my dad."* What a powerful statement from a trusting daughter. Both girls showed extreme bravery. Even though they didn't fully understand what their actions were accomplishing, they trusted their parents who put them in the situation.

Chosen Woman, times that require extreme bravery are ordered by your Father. He knows your skills and strengths and He positions you to stand in those difficult moments trusting in Him. The question is, "What will you do with what He has given you?" Will you solider on calmly like little Ruby? Will you declare your trust in your Father's protective presence like Pam? Only you can choose how you will respond. Proverbs 24:10 (CSB) warns us, *"If you do nothing in a difficult time, your strength is limited."*

Do you want to be a woman of unlimited strength of character? Do you want to be a woman whose trust in God is displayed in her courageous actions? If so, then look to formidable times as opportunities to shine bravely for Jesus.

On a scale of **1-10** (1=barely and 10=strongly) **rate your general level of trust in God's plan for your life. Circle your answer.**

1   2   3   4   5   6   7   8   9   10

How confident are your that God has designed the best possible plan for your life? Do you feel God knows you best and places you in situations that cause you to grow into the woman He destined you to be?

On a scale of 1-10 (1=timid and 10=brave) rate your general level of bravery. Circle your answer.

1   2   3   4   5   6   7   8   9   10

Why did you give yourself the rating that you did? Give an example that validates your answer.

Compare the two ratings.
Do they speak more of your trust in yourself or your trust in Him?

Read Proverbs 3:5-6.

More and more we see our culture shifting away from the instructions that God's Word supplies for daily living. We are constantly challenged to conform to the world's way of acting and reacting.

Have you ever felt that you had to go against social or current culture norms? Describe a particular situation and how you chose to respond.

God has designed each of us with strengths in our personalities, but He also places resources within "arm's length" of us. These resources are there to complement our strengths and further equip us to walk out our mission.

List at least 5 such resources that complement or strengthen your mission. (For example, people groups such as church, MOPS, or work friends. Maybe interests/ activities such as gardening, pottery, cycling, kick boxing, etc.)

1.

2.

3.

4.

5.

Referring to the above list, have you ever had to "use what you've got" to fulfill something that God has asked you to do? Did any one person or thing in the above list help you feel as if you were acting bravely?

SCRIPTURE REFERENCES: Read Her Story!
Judges 4:1-24; 5:24-26

SIGNATURE:
JAEL [JAY-el: "mountain goat"]

SETTING:
[Date: About 1300 B.C.] At the time, Israel was at war with the Canaanites. Canaan was ruled by the King Jaben. God was handing the Israelites over to Jaben as punishment for idolatry. Sisera was the commander of the Canaanite army. He was a powerful and cruel man who oppressed the Israelites for twenty years with the goal of conquering Israel. Israel was in a desperate economic situation. Israel was ruled by Deborah the prophetess and only female judge. Deborah had appointed Barak to lead the Israelite army.

BE BRAVE ENOUGH TO CHANGE THE WORLD! Don't diminish God's calling based on location or circumstances. Throughout the Bible we read of women who simply took a deep breath and said "Yes." Changing the world starts with *the world around you.* Sometimes we want to make it more complicated thinking surely bravery must be associated with *grand displays* in strength of character.

The KJV Dictionary defines bravery as:

> **BRAVERY=** *"An undaunted spirit, fearlessness of danger or dignity of mind which despises meanness and cruelty."*

With this in mind we could say bravery is acting on what you know is right while maintaining a determined posture in the face of opposing pressure. Chosen woman, we can read the accounts of how our biblical heroines stood fast and we be encouraged by their bravery. However, we must understand it was not their spunk or feisty attitudes that steadied them. They placed their trust in the Lord and He proved repeatedly that He was their salvation. He was their present help in time of need. Each biblical account makes it clear, the Most-High was the real hero, working through His daughters in ways that were unique. Esther could not have stood in Deborah's place. Jael was not meant to live Hanna's story. Just like these ladies, you and I are to stand in our story with confidence in the Lord and trust He has designed us for the daunting moments that come to everyone's doorstep. Be encouraged today! You are just as Chosen as Jael or any of her courageous counterparts. When your time comes, you will be ready!

The Psalmist encouraged himself in the following passage:

"Wait patiently for the Lord.
Be BRAVE and COURAGEOUS.
Yes, wait patiently for the Lord."

Psalm 26:14 NLT

God does not shy away from using women that most people would overlook or honestly discount! God has used the most tainted and flawed people from the very beginning, and He continues to do it today.

Read Genesis 38- "TAMAR"

This is the story of Tamar. Perhaps you have heard her name mentioned, usually it is attached to notoriety. Her story is rich in ancient societal norms that can be difficult in which to relate. We can, however, understand that hers is a story of a family fractured by sin. The choices of others left her abandoned. The system failed her, but God did not. She was brave. And although her desperate actions may shock us, God turned her story around and allowed blessing in the end.

Judah, a son of Israel, had two sons who were men of questionable character. The eldest was Tamar's husband and his wicked choices resulted in death. Scripture shows his brother to be a man with no respect for the commands of his father and his choices denied Tamar her rightful blessing of providing an heir for her husband and led to her brother-in-law's untimely death. There was a third brother who could've provided a solution, but Judah's fear caused him to deceive and abandon Tamar.

Tamar was prevented from taking her rightful place in Judah's legacy, but she was determined not to cower to her circumstances.

As if this story was not complicated and shocking enough, Tamar devised a plan to make herself whole in a way we consider extremely inappropriate. She tricked Judah, her father-in-law, into sleeping with her. Remember, this was their culture not ours, and the Holy Spirit did not inspire her story into Scripture to teach us this as a means to justify the end! Quite the opposite. The lesson is- God wins in the end! He wins by having a planned purpose available to all, even the abandoned and manipulated. He wins by utilizing people just like you and me to accomplish His will on the earth. We must remind ourselves that the people we read about in Scripture are real people with real problems who chose to serve a real God with real answers! They are not characters who are made up by an author.

Write down a situation where you have been let down. Describe how that made you feel and what it made you think of yourself.

Tamar had two children by Judah (her Father-in-law), Perez and Zerah. Even though her whole world fell apart, Tamar acted honorably, she really did! I know that is hard to fathom. When Judah realized that he had delivered a great injustice on this young woman it was he who was repentant. In Genesis 38:27 he exclaimed *"She is more righteous than I am."* Her bravery created an opportunity for God's promises to Judah to be fulfilled.

Guard your heart! Tamar did not act vengefully, but righteously. She did not set out to shame Judah, only to claim what was hers and God rewarded her with a legacy all her own. Keep that in mind. Bravery is not revenge.

Consider times when you were treated wrongly and it called for brave action. How did you respond? Were you gracious or vengeful? Were you a able to be forgiving or have you been holding a bitter grudge? **Give an example.**

Read Ruth 4 (take note of verse 12 and verses 18-22).
The name Perez means *"breakthrough."* The Lord literally gave Tamar her *breakthrough*! Tamar, who was widowed, abandoned, mistreated, and manipulated was blessed by God to be part of the greatest legacy of all, the genealogy of Jesus. We do not know how a moment of bravery will affect our life or the lives of others. We do know we serve a God we can trust to use our wiliness to stand for Him and change our world!

Read Ruth 4:12 and Matthew 1:3.

Why did Scripture make sure to include Tamar in the declaration of blessing to Boaz and the genealogy of Jesus?

Do you believe the Lord desires to make your story that impactful? Y/N

What evidence do you have to support your answer?

Have you ever thought your life was marked by too many imperfections, or lack of educations and experience to be used by God?

Read Luke 7:36-50- "THE SINFUL WOMAN"

Another woman Scripture highlights for her bravery and extravagant devotion is found in the gospel of Luke. She is simply known as the "Sinful Woman." Her story can teach us how God can position the most unlikely soul with the most unique tools that call for reckless bravery. Her story is sweet yet scandalous. She had a reputation in her community and was not a stranger to public shame. Yet she seized an opportunity and followed her heart to the feet of Jesus, and that, Chosen Woman, is BRAVE.

What do you think the people in her town said about her? Why do you think that did not hinder her from coming to Jesus?

After the woman began to pour her tears and oil on the feet of Jesus, the room filled with disparaging toward her, by the host of the dinner no less. Jesus, perceiving these thoughts, challenged the man. The Lord used this teachable moment to tell a parable.

Read verses 40-43.

How does the parable relate to what was happening in the room?

How does this parable relate to your own experience with Jesus?

Read verses 44-46. List the actions of the host toward Jesus.

1.

2.

3.

In contrast, how did the Sinful Woman show extravagant bravery in her expression of love for Jesus?

1.

2.

3.

What was the result of her actions?

Read verse 50.
Does that statement describe your standing with God?   Y / N

I pray you answered yes. Jesus approves of your love toward Him. His response to our love is extravagant forgiveness. The woman used her tears and precious oil to express the depth of that love.

How does knowing Jesus approves of and welcomes your love and worship influence how extravagantly brave you are in pouring yourself out to Him?

We MUST get out of our "religious bubble" and see people, truly see people the way that God does! We can sit in our churches and say with our mouths, "no one is too far from God that He can't rescue them!" But it is a complete next step to have an expectation for God to USE those same people that He just rescued, even amid their brokenness!

Has there been a season in your life where you had to trust "Heavenly Rules" over earthly religious rules? Describe it.

Charles Spurgeon compared Sisera to sin saying,

"Instead of just praying for sin to flee, you drive a stake in it and KILL It!"

Jael's story is an example of how we should fight spiritual battles. We know our battle isn't with flesh and blood (Ephesians 6:12). We destroy sin's power over us with the tools the Lord has given us. There is no greater tool that His Word. When you learn what the Word says about how to navigate the difficult situations in your life, you are carrying the most powerful weapon you will ever need.

Read 2 Timothy 2:7 (NKJV). Fill in the blanks below:

*For God has not given us a _____ _____
_____ , but of _____ , and of
_____ and of a _____ _____.*

Perhaps this scripture is so familiar it seems repetitive but if you will commit it to your heart and skillfully recall it in times of attack, you will find it a powerful truth against the devil's lies. Fear and timidity are the exact opposite of bravery. Fear will put you in a choke hold and paralyze you.

Read Isaiah 43:1-3.

Why does God tell us not to fear?

What are the three conditions that would cause us difficulty?

What do each of the following conditions represent in your life?

- Waters—

- Rivers—

- Fire—

What is the Lord's promise regarding each condition?

- Waters—

- Rivers—

- Fire—

Read the following Scriptures:
- 1 Chronicles 28:20
- Deuteronomy 31:6
- Joshua 1:9

What is the one obvious promise God wants His children to know?

Finally, *what is in your hand?*
We all have something we can use when the enemy comes to trouble us. We have examined the lives of unsuspecting housewives, young girls, and wronged women. Each of them brought something to the fight that was divinely placed in their   personality or proximity. You will never engage your enemy ill-equipped. Each of us has something that is unique to our design.

Write down what you possess to fight the enemy—list one thing from your community (external), one thing from your personality (internal), and one trait you inherited at salvation (spiritual).

External _____

Internal_____

Spiritual_____

Fun Facts: ABOUT JAEL

♦ Jael means "*Wild Mountain Goat*"- Can you imagine having a name with that meaning? A wild mountain goat is said to be comparatively more tendinous than a domestic goat, and they are willing to fight for what they believe to be their's.

♦ Jael was the wife of Hebner who was a Kenite. This was the same ethnic group that Jethro, Moses father-in-law was from.

SIMPLIFY: Personal Application

Take Jael as an example to trust what you have been given. You are strong, equipped, and called to be used by God. Refuse to let manmade qualifications deter you from your calling. When the Holy Spirit begins to tug at your heart, just say Yes and keep saying Yes!

Pause and take inventory. If you sing, give it to God. If you write, give it to God. If you teach, give it to God. If you host, give it to God. What do you have that you are skilled in and brave enough to say, "Here I am Lord, with what I have in my hand, use me?"

Are you struggling with sin such as pride, envy, or lust? Anything that is between you and the heavenly Father? Approach it like Jael did, with bravery, drive a stake in it and KILL it!

SUPPLICATION: Prayer Focus

Dear God, I trust you! I trust that you have my past, my present, and my future in your hands. Throughout Scripture, I see that you used women just like me to make an impact for your kingdom. You did it then and you are doing it now. Forgive me for doubting or disqualifying the gifts and talents that you specifically placed inside of me. I have been chosen to be brave and I say "yes" as you direct. I am committed to changing the world by changing the world around me, for your glory and honor! In Jesus name!
Amen

STORY BOARD: Journal Notes

What was revealed to you about the Character of God through HER STORY?

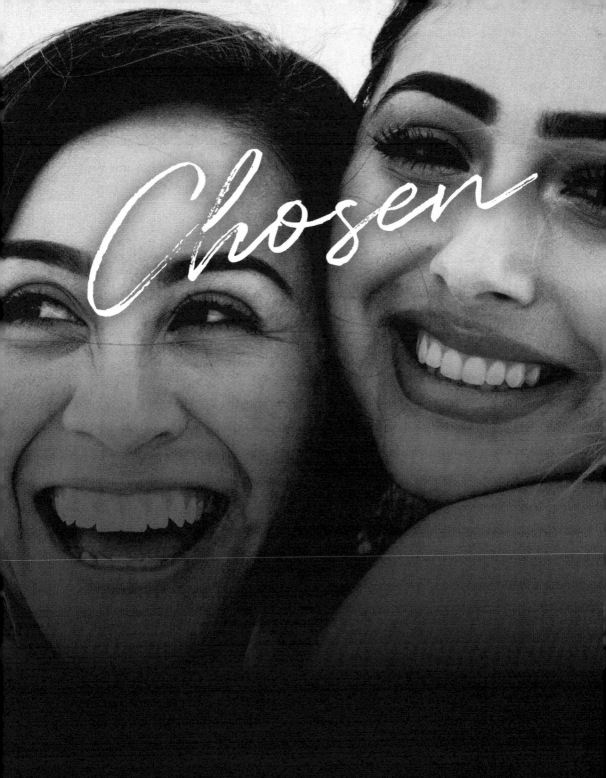

Chosen

TO SHARE
THE GOSPEL!

HER STORY

The Samaritan Woman

By Olivia Carter

"Now from that city many of the Samaritans believed in Him because of the word of the woman who testified, 'He told me all the things that I have done.' So, when the Samaritans came to Jesus, they were asking Him to stay with them; and He stayed there two days. Many more believed because of His word; and they were saying to the woman, 'It is no longer because of what you said that we believe, for we have heard for ourselves and know that this One truly is the Savior of the world.'"
JOHN 4:39-42 (NASB)

Whether internally or externally imposed, I imagine most of us have felt disregarded before. Maybe we were actually outcast by someone we hoped would value us. Maybe our deepest insecurities cause us to disregard and isolate ourselves. Either way, the feeling cast aside or looked over is a difficult feeling that many of us have experienced, and through this mutual experience, we might be able to find a "Samaritan Woman" in each of us.

> ## We must be willing to have redemptive conversations with those who are different than us.

CONVERSATIONS MATTER

The story of the Samaritan Woman is such a significant biblical encounter. This conversation that started as a regular errand for the woman ended up changing the course of biblical history and was a catalyst from which many Samaritans heard the gospel. When I read this story, I see so much of what we experience today in our world. While there certainly have been more divided times in history, we haven't had access to the opinions of everyone that we know like we do today. I know there are times that I can be tempted to write people off because they perceive the issues we face differently than I do. However, when I read the words of this story, I am reminded of the power of a simple conversation, and how genuine care for another person can break through what feels to be like an impossible barrier. When I read the words of this story, I am reminded that Jesus came for the outcasts of society. He came for those who are overlooked, demeaned, and disregarded. While He also came for those who may not fall into those categories, He does not place us in different categories of importance. This story should remind us that Jesus loves all, and we should too. He doesn't abide by the social classifications that we create, but pierces through that and speaks straight to the heart of those who are willing to hear. We must be willing to have redemptive conversations with those who are different than us. Jesus broke the barriers of inequality with a simple conversation. He is our great example. Conversations matter.

COMPASSION MATTERS

When I read this story of the Samaritan Woman, I am also reminded of my own sin. While it can be so easy for me to try and disqualify myself, I am not powerful enough to do so. The Samaritan Woman certainly did not have a simple journey when it came to relationships. While I don't know the specifics of her situation, I can imagine that there were some situations she put herself in that likely were not the best for her. However, even knowing that, Jesus calls out what it is He knows she has been walking through, but He doesn't shame her for it. He doesn't disqualify her from being able to share the gospel, but rather uses that very same pain to demonstrate that He truly is the Messiah. When we choose to surrender our pain and sin to the Lord, what we'll find is that He doesn't use that as a basis on which to condemn us, but rather He uses that very same pain to show us exactly who He is. Our sin does not disqualify us from our calling, nor does it disqualify anyone else. I think it's easy for us to grasp onto this concept and believe it to be true for ourselves and those we love. However, it applies to the person that you don't like so much as well. It applies to the relative that you can barely stand to be around. It applies to the person who has hurt you. It applies to the person who always has something negative to say. Let that truth not only help you to have compassion for yourself, but for those that it might be difficult to empathize with. Compassion matters.

> # When we are faithful to share our story,
> # God is faithful to do what we cannot.

COURAGE MATTERS

Lastly, when I read this story, I am reminded of the power of my own story. While I can see myself in the Samaritan Woman, I have my own unique journey through which God has proven Himself faithful. It provides great encouragement to me to look back and see how the Lord has been there even when I have tried to run from Him. However, my story is not only meant for my encouragement, but also to demonstrate to others the power of God in my life. When the Samaritan Woman returned to her city, she said to them *"He told me all the things that I have done,"* and it was from her testimony that this city had opened themselves up to the gospel. This took great courage! Remarkably, this didn't stop with her story. The scripture later states that the people in her city then heard for themselves from Jesus and knew that He was the Savior of the world. When we are faithful and courageous to share our story, God is faithful to do what we cannot. Courage matters.

> # Your story is your greatest message!

The story of the Samaritan Woman is so powerful because it shows us that God chooses those who have been cast out from society, those who have endured great pain because of their sin, and He uses that to further His mission in the world. It can be so easy for us to believe that our story is not significant or dramatic enough to be worth telling, but that couldn't be further from the truth.

Your story is your greatest message, one that God will use to speak to the hearts of those who do not yet know Him. Just like the Samaritan Woman, each of us have been chosen to share the gospel, and it starts with our story.

Life Lessons:

1. **CONVERSATION MATTERS:** Jesus has a great love and compassion for the world, and so should we. Jesus sat and spent time with a person of low social standing. Her gender, race, and marital status may have caused her to be disregarded by many. However, Jesus spoke so directly with her as equal conversational partners. If anyone has a reason to not treat someone as "equal," it's Jesus! And how often do we, flawed human beings look at others as if they are beneath us? Rather than looking at the Samaritan Woman as she had been looked at by many, He sat with her. Our conversation with the broken matters.

2. **COMPASSION MATTERS:** Jesus sees all, yet He still has compassion for us. I can only imagine how uncomfortable it might have felt for the Samaritan Woman to have a stranger call out her sin. I know I would be! However, even though Jesus knew what she had done, He never shamed her or condemned her. In fact, He empowered her to live rightly. Jesus loves us and calls us regardless of our past. Let's move forward keeping that in mind so that we can have grace and compassion for ourselves and others. How we sit with the broken speaks louder than how we sit with the great. Compassion matters.

3. **COURAGE MATTERS:** It is so interesting to see how many of us look at our trials and see ways that it could prevent us from pursuing the call of God on our lives. However, it is very often that same brokenness that God uses to direct us in our calling. We should not be ashamed of our story. After her encounter with Jesus, the Samaritan Woman was not ashamed either, in fact, she shared boldly what Jesus had done in their meeting. As difficult as it may be, let's embody this same courage to share our story. We never know what God will do when we surrender our testimony. Courage matters.

YOUR STORY: Personal Reflection

"INSIGNIFICANT" means =
too small or unimportant to be worth consideration.

As you read this definition, you may feel a little defined yourself. Everyone has felt *"too something"* at one time or another, but I assure you no one is insignificant to the Lord. Each of you has been chosen to share His gospel through your story of redemption.

How has the feeling of being disregarded or overlooked affected you?

What ways has God comforted you in moments that you felt like an outcast (uninvited, or rejected)? This is part of your story!

What scripture can you cling to in times of feeling this way?

There is a seemingly insignificant woman mentioned in Genesis chapter 30. Her name is Zilpah, handmaid to Leah. Zilpah had two sons with Leah's husband Jacob. Her sons were raised as Leah's. As we would see it today, they were a dysfunctional family. When you feel insignificant, remember God's plan for you is not based on anything but His perfect love for you.

Read Genesis 30: 12-13
What was the name of Zilpah's second-born son?

Read Luke 2:36-38. Fill in the graph below:

Who is the prophetess in this story?	What tribe did she descend from?	How did she share the gospel that day at the temple?

Zilpah's station was too low, and Anna was too old (in the eye of their cultures), but God used their stories to help spread the gospel.

Fill in the blank.

I feel too _____ to share my story.

Read 2 Corinthians 10:4-5

Rewrite the above sentence in the space below. As you write, picture your redeemed self, pulling that statement down as it tries to dominate your thoughts. Now strike a line through it, scribble over it, blot is out with markers. Do whatever you can to "demolish" it.

I feel too _____ to share my story.

God has chosen you to share the gospel and He has made sure NOTHING will stand in your way!

FEELING	PROMISE FROM SCRIPTURE
Unwanted, rejected, not good enough...	*"For you are a people holy to the Lord your God. Out of all peoples on the face of the earth, the Lord has chosen you to be his treasured possession"* Deuteronomy 14:2 NIV.

Keep this promise somewhere that you can see it often as a reminder.

HIS STORY: Digging Deeper

SCRIPTURE REFERENCES:
John 4:6-42

SETTING:
[Date: About A.D. 30] While she is never named, the "Woman at the Well" or the "Samaritan Woman," she has one of the most significant encounters with Jesus recorded in Scripture. This is special not only because of the details of this encounter, but the participants. Despised for her race, oppressed for her gender, the Samaritan Woman represents the disregarded and demeaned. In her day the Jew had a deep enmity for the Samaritans. They believed to be considered unpure half-breeds. The enmity had so long been established that a Jew would walk a great distance out of their way to go around Samaria, rather than through it, just to prevent any unwanted encounter.

Chosen Woman, you are most definitely called to share the gospel. It starts with your story and ends with Jesus' free gift to all. Let God develop a hunger for His Word, the Living Water, inside of you. Don't be intimidated if you don't have a full grasp of Scripture. We all start in the same place- In front of a Man (Jesus) who looks past our mistakes and insignificance and welcomes us with this declaration,

> *"You don't have to wait any longer, the Anointed One is here speaking with you—I am the One you're looking for."*
> John 4:26 TPT

Read John 4:7-42

Why was the Samaritan Woman surprised that Jesus had asked her for a drink? What does this say about Jesus?

At the time of the exchange, there was great animosity between Jewish people and Samaritan people. Women were also socially disregarded and perceived to be less than. This conversation with the woman at the well was controversial in many ways.

Who in your life have you overlooked or discarded? (Maybe it was purposeful, or maybe it was not purposeful but came from a cultural upbringing that may have had more of an impact on you than you thought).

It may not be for reasons similar to that of the Samaritan Woman, but we all know people whose differences make it difficult for us to relate to.

This week think of a way that you can step outside of your typical social circle and connect with someone much different than yourself. Share your thoughts.

The woman asked a question (4:9,10). Given the antagonism that existed between Jews and Samaritans the question could have been predicted. The woman was surprised that Jesus would speak to her, much less display a willingness to drink from a cup handed to him by a Samaritan.

Jesus redirected her attention to the "gift of God" (4:10). The real answer to the woman's question (and to our questions) could be found in the identity of the One who spoke to her. Jesus was the One who came bringing "living water."

"LIVING WATER" = meant running water,
such as that which comes from an active flowing stream.

Only "living water" could be used in the baths taken in Judaism to purify a person who was unclean. Christ has come with that same gift of God that would purify believers from all sin.

What does Jesus say the water that He provides will become? What significance does this have in your life?

Jesus tells the woman that a "time is coming and has now come when the true worshipers will worship the Father in Spirit and in truth."

What does it look like for you to worship the Father in Spirit and truth in your daily life?

What does Jesus say his food is to the disciples? How can this truth impact our lives?

How did Jesus use the knowledge He had of the Samaritan Woman's life to further His mission? What does this say about Jesus?

Jesus says to His disciples that *"the one who reaps is receiving wages and gathers fruit for eternal life, so that the one who sows and the one who reaps may rejoice together."*

What can we gather about the work we do on earth from this statement?

What were the reactions of the disciples when they came to the well and saw Jesus speaking with the Samaritan Woman? Why do you suppose they acted that way?

The Samaritan Woman told Jesus that she knew the Messiah was coming. He responded with *"I am He, the One speaking to you."*

Jesus was the promised Messiah. Look up these Scriptures:

LOOK UP THESE SCRIPTURES:	Who Proclaimed Jesus as Messiah in each of these verses?
Luke 2:10-11	
John 1:35-41	
Matthew 3:16-17	
Acts 2:36	
Philippians 2:9-11	

Read Isaiah 61 in Luke 4.
What was Jesus saying here?

Return to John 4: 28-30

After hearing Jesus declare Himself as the long-awaited Messiah and telling the woman things about herself that He could not have known unless they were revealed to Him by God, **immediately** she went back to her city and told the people of what Jesus had done. Once she knew who He was, she wasted no time to share her story!

This woman at the well discovered something in accepting Christ that she had yearned for. Jesus gave her the unconditional acceptance and love that we all ache for. What the woman may have sought in promiscuous sex she found through a pure faith in Jesus. And so can we today.

The woman whose guilt had led her to avoid others, now sought them out. The woman who tried to hide her sins was now open to them: "He told me all things that I ever did!" (vs. 29). Cleansed and transformed, she focused on Christ rather than on herself. She became a vibrant and successful witness for Jesus Christ.

What can we learn from this?

Continue reading- verse 39-42

The Samaritan people welcomed Jesus into their city and into their homes.
After learning more about the social climate at the time, particularly between Jewish people and Samaritan people, what truths can we gain from their eagerness to take Him in?

According to 2 Corinthians 5:18, God did two things for us through Christ.
What are they?

According to 2 Corinthians 5:19, *who can receive this reconciliation and who is qualified to share the Gospel message of Christ?*

We are all called to be Ambassadors of Christ.

An "*AMBASSADOR*" = is one that has been granted authority
to speak on behalf of a ruler/leader and given a specific message
from that ruler/leader to share with others.

Read 2 Corinthians 5:20.
According to this verse, as Ambassadors of Christ who is making the appeal through us and what have we been sent to say?

Read Mark 1:17 and Mark 6:7

Which disciples were called to evangelize?

SIMPLIFY: Personal Application

Regardless of who we are, what we have done, or how we are perceived, God has chosen us to share the gospel. While this call may seem overwhelming and daunting for those of us who don't identify as "preachers," God has already equipped us with a great message that He will use to bring the lost home: our stories. When we can be tempted to disqualify ourselves or disqualify others from sharing the gospel, let us be reminded of this encounter at the well. In the middle of great cultural, religious, and racial divide, Jesus sat with a woman who would be overlooked by many, spoke into her life, and empowered her to share the gospel.

I WILL...

- **WRITE** the names of three people who need Jesus.
- **PRAY** for them everyday and love them like Jesus.
- **LOOK** for opportunities to share Jesus with them.

MY THREE:

1. _____
2. _____
3. _____

SHARE YOUR STORY WITH US!

There is power in a story! And when someone comes to saving faith in Jesus Christ, it impacts their eternity! So we want to celebrate with you. If you would like to share the story of how you've reached someone for Christ, simply visit **pcg.org/impacteternity.**

SUPPLICATION: Prayer Focus

God, I pray that you would humble me so that I may see myself and others through your eyes. Help me to see past my own biases and insecurities so that I can boldly proclaim the work you have done in my life. When fear comes, fill me with your truth through your Living water. When judgment arises, remind me of how far you have brought me. Lord, may I go from this place, as your CHOSEN daughter, ready to share the Gospel message and my glorious salvation story. Amen.

STORY BOARD: Journal Notes

What was revealed to you about the Character of God through HER STORY?

YOU HAVE A *Chosen* STORY TO SHARE

Why share my story?

- **Your story is the best tool you have to spread the Good News of Jesus Christ.** It is personal, it is real, and it is that one thing you know the most about—your own experience with God.

How do I share my story?

- **Write your story down.**
    - *Pray and Ask the Holy Spirit for help.* Writing your story down will help you organize your thoughts to communicate more clearly.

- **Here is a helpful guide line to start with:**
    - *Who I Was-* Describe what life was like before you met Jesus, (share details as you are comfortable, every opportunity is different).
    - *Who I Am-* Tell how you have changed since Jesus became your Lord. It's not about what you've given up but what you've gained!
    - *Who I Am Becoming-* Share what God is doing in and through your, or what direction God is taking your life now and in the future?

- **How long should it be?**
    - You should be able to tell your story in *3 minutes or less.* Good stories should be engaging and concise. All of Jesus' parables were this way and we would love to tell stories like Jesus.

Write a short version of your redemption story below.

_____

_____

_____

_____

_____

_____

_____

_____

_____

"For you are

a people

holy to the Lord

your God.

Out of all peoples

on the face

of the earth,

the Lord has

CHOSEN YOU

to be His

treasured

possession.

Deuteronomy 14:2 NIV.

Chosen

FOR
MINISTRY!

HER STORY

Priscilla

By Kathy Whited

"Now a Jew named Apollos, a native of Alexandria, came to Ephesus. He was an eloquent man, competent in the Scriptures. He had been instructed in the way of the Lord. And being fervent in spirit, he spoke and taught accurately the things concerning Jesus, though he knew only the baptism of John. He began to speak boldly in the synagogue, but when Priscilla and Aquila heard him, they took him aside and explained to him the way of God more accurately. And when he wished to cross Achaia, the brothers encouraged him and wrote to the disciples to welcome him. When he arrived, he greatly helped those who through grace believed, for he powerfully refuted the Jews in public, showing by the Scriptures that the Christ was Jesus."
ACTS 18:24-28 (ESV)

Out of difficult circumstances there can come great things. The year 2020 (a Global Covid Pandemic) was very difficult for many. During this frightening time many were filled with questions of "why Lord," or "what are we to do now?" No one would know how this was going to work out. Yet God has brought purpose in our path. Amidst our fear of the unknown, sorrow, loneliness, and pain, God was with us all.

"God is our refuge and strength, always ready to help in times of trouble."
Psalm 46:1 NLT

In October 2020 I found myself presented with an unlikely opportunity. Feeling led by the Lord I applied for a ministry position. Even though I did not qualify with all of the requirements that were needed, the Lord chose me to represent Him as a Chaplain in our local hospital. This allowed me to shine the light of Jesus to the hurting, broken, and oppressed in a new way. This opportunity placed me in a position to lead others to the Great Physician. Regardless of our past or present circumstances, God has a divinely chosen plan and purpose for every one of His daughters. He has uniquely gifted each of us with talents and gifts. When we surrender whole heartedly to His purpose, He will make the way clear for us. He will give us favor and open doors of opportunity. When we make room for Him, He makes room for us!

"A man's (woman's) gift makes room for him (her) and
brings him (her) before the great."
Proverbs 18:16 ESV

Chosen woman of God, He has a chosen plan and purpose for YOU!

COMMITMENT IN MINISTRY
Priscilla must have felt some feelings of uncertainty as she left the familiarity of her home for a new path, not knowing what was to come next. Although her future seemed to be a mystery to her and her husband, God had a plan. She was a woman of the Word, familiar with the Scriptures. When her circumstances and environment changed, it did not change her commitment to the Lord. Moving into unknown territory for the purpose of ministry took courage. She was a hospitable homemaker and a tent maker by trade. She was never mentioned alone, but always with her husband Aquila, as a couple. She was committed to her husband, her home, her community and most importantly to her Lord and His Word. Priscilla was hospitable and opened her home, not only to the Apostle Paul for an extended period of time, but many more in helping to establish a church. She was willing to work with her hands in tent making and preparing food for others. She was also willing to be a part of a church plant in the city of

Ephesus, a city that was still new to her. She was committed to the Lord to the extent that she was willing to step into the unknown and fully trust His plan for her life.

TEACHABILITY IN MINISTRY

Priscilla first had to follow the Lord and the pattern of leadership that was placed in her life by Him. He had chosen her for a specific purpose, and she would lead by example but first she had to be submissive to learn from others. Before Priscilla could teach others, she had to be teachable herself. As a Jew she would have been trained in the Old Testament Scriptures from an early age; submitting to the counsel of others. When Paul came and stayed with her and Aquila, undoubtedly, they learned a clearer understanding of the Gospel from him. Paul taught each week in the synagogue and I'm sure he shared with this dedicated couple around the dinner table many times about the things of Jesus and the baptism in the Holy Spirit. No matter the age or stage of ministry we are engaged in, we must remain teachable and pliable in the hands of the Lord as He uses others to help us.

> # God took what Priscilla extended in Godly leadership to one life, and multiplied it for the many.

MULTIPLICATION IN MINISTRY

Among the many that Priscilla and her husband ministered to was a young man who would become a great evangelist and share the Gospel of Jesus Christ. In helping to further equip that one young man, Priscilla was able to touch so many lives. We later witness in the Scriptures such a powerful influence that this young, exuberant preacher had— His name was Apollos. As she and Aquila were in the Synagogue, they heard Apollos preaching the good news of Jesus. He was a dynamic public speaker who spoke with passion and accuracy. They listened intently to him. He was from Alexandria, which was known for its scholarly learning and world-famous library. They recognized a need to share with him about the baptism of the Holy Spirit and the way of God more accurately (Acts 18:26). She and her husband took him aside privately. They did not allow the fact that Apollos had come from a very educated background to hinder them. After mentoring and teaching him, they sent him off to Corinth with a welcoming letter to preach powerfully with a deeper knowledge of the way of Jesus. God took what Priscilla extended in Godly leadership to one life and multiplied it for the many. During this time period it was unlikely that a woman would mentor a young man that was not her own child, and yet the Lord made room for her and used her unique voice to give guidance, encouragement, and a depth in the Word that would   propel the proclamation of the gospel into faraway places. Because of her willingness to follow the plan and purpose of God in ministry, many lives were forever transformed by the power of the Holy Spirit for the glory of God! God took all of her gifts and used them for His glory on the chosen path He had for her.

LIFE LESSONS:

1. **COMMITMENT IN MINISTRY:** Every man and woman is called to be a minister of the gospel. God is equipping all of us to lead, mentor and teach others in some way. For example: Stay-at-home mothers are training their children and equipping them for the days ahead. Leading, mentoring and teaching your little ones is of vital importance. Through one life many are influenced. You may be a single or married woman who has no biological children, but the Lord has given you spiritual sons and daughters to mentor and teach. In your workplace you are chosen to lead by example in your words and actions. Be assured someone is taking note of your life.

2. **TEACHABILITY IN MINISTRY:** Teachability in ministry is a must. We should be ever-learning in every area of our lives. Historical evidence shows that Priscilla was a Roman Jew from an aristocratic family. As a member of a higher class, her roman education involved her in higher learning of Greek rhetoric and philosophy. This would set her up to be a great communicator. She was teachable in her formative years and obviously remained teachable in her spiritual formation given her and Aquila's close friendship with Paul the Apostle. But in order to be a noted teacher in Acts 18:26, she had to first be teachable. Leaders are first learners. Make it a goal to learn everything you can from trusted mentors and pastors. As you do, you will grow exponentially and it will benefit everyone to whom you minister, whether in your own home or abroad.

3. **MULTIPLICATION IN MINISTRY:** Priscilla shows us by example that what we do for the Lord makes more of an impact than what we can see today. You may feel the nudging of the Lord to teach and preach His Word publicly or simply to mentor those around you. We see in Priscilla's example that she

was already full of the Scriptures so that when He called her to mentor, she was ready. When we remain in the Word and fellowship with our Lord in prayer, we are always ready to do what He has called us to do! As we step into His plan, the ministry that He has for us will multiply and reach more people than we could ever dream of reaching! Intentionally pour yourself into those around you and you will find that multiplication in ministry happens naturally!

YOUR STORY: Personal Reflection

Abraham looked at the stars, Joshua looked at the walls of Jericho, and Esther looked at the doors that led to the throne room of King Xerxes. God has called the most unlikely candidates to lead the most extra-ordinary lives. For centuries, the first response to that call is to take a critical assessment of ourselves and declare we are not worthy, qualified, or equipped to step into the possibilities He has planned for us. God's answer to our concerns is always the same, "trust and obey." When Joshua inherited the weighty mantel after the death of Moses, the Lord encouraged him with these words:

"Be strong and courageous, for you are the one who will lead these people to possess all the land I swore to their ancestors I would give them. Be strong and very courageous. Be careful to obey all the instructions Moses gave you. Do not deviate from them, turning either to the right or to the left. Then you will be successful in everything you do. Study this Book of Instruction continually. Meditate on it day and night so you will be sure to obey everything written in it. Only then will you prosper and succeed in all you do. This is my command—be strong and courageous! Do not be afraid or discouraged. For the Lord your God is with you wherever you go."

Joshua 1:6-9 NLT.

When was the last time you trusted the Lord's leading with a circumstance that was outside of your control to change?

Have you completely surrendered all your gifts and talents to His purpose, knowing that all we do as a daughter of the King matters?

Is there an individual in your life that God is leading you to mentor, lead, or teach? How is God calling you to be a minister for Him?

It can be easy to allow our longings to cause us to lose sight of God's leadings. We know He has created us according to plan and equipped us for every assignment.

Proverbs 3:5 TPT says:
"Trust in the Lord completely, and do not rely on your own opinions. With all your heart rely on him to guide you, and he will lead you in every decision you make."

List the talents/gifts you wish you had.

    1.

    2.

    3.

    4.

    5.

List the talents/gifts you feel God has empowered you with? *(If you're not sure what to write, ask a woman (or women) from your study group to help you identify how God is growing you.)*

    1.

    2.

    3.

    4.

    5.

Which list better represents the woman you are?

Priscilla's example shows us that as we continue to follow the Lord's leading, He will show us the next step. She could not see all that God had for her to do ahead of time. She had to trust His leading over her longings. She may have longed to stay in the familiar and not step out in the unknown, but as she trusted His timing the picture of His plan and purpose became clearer. She had a working knowledge of the Scriptures and was ready to teach at any given moment. God will always give us room to lead, mentor, and teach others, but we must first be prepared. Abraham Lincoln said,

"I will prepare and someday my chance will come!"

God never makes mistakes. According to Proverbs 3:5, 6 what should you do develop trust in God's leading as opposed to your longings?

Are you teachable to those who are leading you? Do you walk in a spirit of humility?

**If God has called you to it,
He has prepared you for it!
He will use every gift, natural talent,
and life experience to accomplish
His will in your life.**

SCRIPTURE REFERENCES: Read Her Story!
Acts 18:1-26; Romans 16:3-4, 1 Corinthians 16:19, 2 Timothy 4:19

SIGNATURE:
PRISCILLA [prih-SIL-uh: meaning unknown]— Priscilla is often called Prisca by the Apostle Paul.

SETTING:
[About A.D. 50] Priscilla was a Jew who formerly had lived in Rome with her husband, Aquila. They had been forced from their home by Emperor Claudius who had expelled all Jews. They had been victims of riots and persecution and had fled to Corinth. The Apostle Paul was staying with them. They went with him on his next journey and remained in Ephesus.

God loves His daughters. His Word includes story after story of women He chose to change the world. Every woman He chose was like a beautiful jewel who sparkled in her setting. We must let the Word buff and polish us until we, like our Biblical sisters, shine in our God-ordained environment. Remember, you don't have any doubt or fear that the women in scripture did not also experience. The same Father that called, qualified, and encouraged them is with you today!

Fun Facts: About Priscilla

♦ Priscilla is often thought to have been the first example of a female preacher or teacher in early church history.

♦ Priscilla is mentioned six times in the New Testament, always with her husband Aquilla. However, four times Priscilla is named first, a peculiarity that indicates she was likely more influential in her church leadership than her husband.

♦ 1 Corinthians 16:19 reveals that Priscilla and Aquilla opened up their home in Ephesus to serve as a church.

♦ Priscilla and Aquilla were tent makers by trade while they were also were very invested in ministry to others.

Fill in the box. Look up the Bible passages. Write down as much information as you can gather about who was ministering, how they ministered, and to whom they were ministering.

Scripture	Who Was Ministering?	How Did She Minister?	Who Received Ministry?
2 Timothy 1:5			
Joel 2:28-29			
Judges 4:4-5			
Exodus 15:20-21			
John 20:16-18			
Acts 21:7-9			

From the above Scriptures what can you gather on how the Lord feels about women who minister through leading, mentoring, and teaching?

Read the following passages: 2 Kings 4:8, Romans 12:13, 1 Timothy 5:10, Hebrews 13:2, I Peter 4:9.

How should the Chosen Women conduct herself in the area of hospitality?

Read 1 Peter 4:9-10 (NIV).
Fill in the blanks from verse 10-11.

"Each of you should use whatever gift you have received to serve others, as faithful stewards of God's grace in its various forms. If anyone speaks, they should do so as one who _____

_____. If anyone serves, they should do so with

_____ , so

that in all things God may be praised through Jesus Christ. To him be the

glory and the power for ever and ever _____."

What should be our objective as we serve (minister to) each other?

Read Romans 16:3-4.
Priscilla was willing to take risks to help the Apostle Paul when he was in hard times and when he was being persecuted.

Who was impacted as a result of the risks Priscilla took?

Describe how you might have the opportunity to take a risk in helping others.

Read 2 Corinthians 10:12.
Knowing that Apollos came from a city of great wisdom could have caused Priscilla to compare how she taught him with that of his other teachers.

What does the Bible say about the danger of comparison?

Priscilla was uniquely positioned for a purpose. She was chosen by God to fulfill His plan for her.

Where do you find yourself currently positioned?

Pause and ask the Lord His purpose for you at this season of your life.

Tent making was a common occupation shared by Paul, Aquila, and Priscilla. It served as a bridge to bring together this divinely appointed friendship. From your circle of influence, think of those whom you have things in common with.

How does your current season provide potential connections that serve as a bridge for Godly influence?

Read Acts 18:26-28.
What can we learn from Aquila and Priscilla about things that should be done privately, and things done publicly?

Read 1 Peter 3:15.
Priscilla's example shows her readiness to share and explain the gospel more accurately. The times she lived in were perilous and perhaps more so for women. That did not negate God's call on her life. She was given grace to navigate her mission with the character of Jesus as her boundaries.

According to this verse, how does it say that this should be done?

How can you put this Scripture into action in your life?

Read Romans 16:3-5.
We see how Aquila and Priscilla dedicated their home to the work of the Lord by becoming a safe place for the early church to meet.

How can you dedicate your home for the work of the Lord? Could you prepare a meal for a newcomer in your church, open your home to a person who needs a place to stay, or help a single mother in keeping her child for a time?

Priscilla stepped out in obedience to the Lord. Despite every voice that said she shouldn't or couldn't, she took her place among the women in the Word and chose to walk in the purpose that Lord chose for her.

What is one area of your life that you need to move from the familiar and step out in faith to His calling?

SIMPLIFY: Personal Application

Gods plan and purpose is that we all become ministers of the gospel. God did not call all to be pastors, preachers, or missionaries, but He did choose each of His children to become ministers of the gospel. We can each share Christ to those in our sphere of influence every day. You have been CHOSEN to lead, mentor, and teach someone in your life.

Let's put Gods plan into action and reach out to someone this week. Share with someone a nugget of the Word of God that the Lord gives you in your own prayer or study time. Speak a word of encouragement to a coworker, friend, or hurting family member. This could be done through a face-to-face connection, over the phone, or even a hand-written card put in the mail. Make it your goal to minister to someone this week! **Pray and ask God for His action plan, He will show you to whom you need to minister.**

SUPPLICATION: Prayer Focus

Lord, You know the plans and purposes that You have chosen for me. You are Creator of all things and You created me with a purpose. Help me to always be ready to minister to others, surrender to Your leading and make room for You above all. Help me to remember that as I follow You, my path will become clearer and more vibrant as I keep my eyes focused upon You. You will equip me each step of the way. As You bless me, help me to be a blessing to others!
In Jesus name, Amen!

STORY BOARD: Journal Notes

What was revealed to you about the Character of God through HER STORY?

Chosen

TO DO
WHATEVER IT TAKES!

HER STORY

Rebekah

Susan Dawn Coffman—

"Now may the God of peace [Who is the Author and the Giver of peace]...equip you with every good thing to carry out His will and strengthen you (complete, perfect) and make you what you ought to be and equip you with everything good that you may carry out His will; [while He Himself] works in you and accomplishes that which is pleasing in His sight, through Jesus Christ (the Messiah); to Whom be the glory forever and ever (to the ages of the ages). Amen ."
HEBREWS 13:21 (AMPC)

Most of us have been in situations where we have had to push ourselves. We just did whatever it took to make it through. Perhaps it was keeping a relationship going, struggling with a health condition, plowing through financial pressures, achieving educational advancement, stepping up to a career demand, experiencing hurts, or simply dealing with everyday challenges. During these times, you have probably heard it said that God will never ask us to do what He will not equip us to do. That teaching is affirmed in our key scripture above, Hebrews 13:21 (AMPC). God's strength will always equip us to fulfill what He has chosen us to do! Let's look at three characteristics that Rebecka held tightly to that will help us navigate through our own life stories.

> ## God's strength will always equip us to fulfill what He has chosen us to do!

GENEROSITY

Little did Rebekah know, as she ended her workday with a last trip to the well, that she was walking into a simple yet fateful test of her character. You see, Abraham had sent his servant Eliezer on a mission to find a bride for his son Isaac, the heir of God's covenant promise. This could not be just any woman, for she would touch destiny and be the matriarch of kings and leaders. At first light of the day she was just a girl, but by days end she was facing the audacious request of a road-weary stranger. What a difference a day can make! Determined to keep his promise to Abraham, Eliezer had travelled 500 miles to Abraham's old hometown. There he positioned himself, with his 10 camels near the city well and asked God to show him the right woman for Isaac based on her response to his request for a drink of water. Eliezer was looking for someone who would not only offer him water but would also offer to bring water to those 10 thirsty camels that were with him. It is estimated that a camel could drink approximately 25 gallons each. Given that the average water jar held only 3 gallons, that would be a daunting task. But Rebekah saw the need, spoken and unspoken. She was not only beautiful, but also wise, compassionate, and evidentially strong enough to be able to complete a task like that at the end of a workday. She did not complain or even call for help. She chose to serve. This is the first glimpse we have into the character of Rebekah. She was generous.

GRIT

The character test at the well would not be the last challenge Rebekah would face. Just when she had proven herself, in character and in deed, she was then asked to leave everything that was familiar to her. She was asked to give herself to a man that she had never met, and to live in a land that was completely foreign to her. Her family expected at least 10 days to say farewell (that seemed fair enough). But Eliezer did not want to wait one moment to see the completion of

God's plan. He asked her to leave immediately. The decision *(CHOICE)* then fell to Rebekah. Her choice would fall between staying a few more days in her home of security and familiarity with family and friends, or to run through the open door to God's plan. At first sight, what woman in her right mind would say yes to leaving with a stranger to marry yet another stranger. The choice could be a difficult one for anyone, but Rebecka ran! She was a woman who understood the downside of staying in her comfort zone, and the blessing of saying "yes" to God. Running into the plan of God with full abandon takes grit, and she had it.

GRACE

We may not fully understand why timing was so important, but scripture indicates that it was. First, we know that Rebekah arrived at the very moment when Isaac was out meditating in the fields. Second, the scripture tells us that Rebekah was deeply loved by Jacob and that "she was a special comfort to him after the death of his mother." After the move to go to where Isaac lived, Rebekah was the one who found herself in a foreign land and would likely never see a single member of her family again. Yet we find her offering comfort to her husband instead of focusing on her own loss and loneliness, that's grace!

It sounds like a fairytale end. But leaving in a moments notice to marry a stranger and finding deep love when she got there was only one chapter of Rebekah's story. The chapters of her story that would follow would include enduring a tortuous 20-year season of barrenness. She was living the chosen life, but with no sign of the promise. Even then, we do not hear Rebekah complain or grow weary. In fact, it is her husband Isaac who pleads with God on her behalf.

God came through and her time of barrenness was over with two sons on the way, but the challenges were not over. The babies struggled within her womb and Rebekah turned to God in her confusion. God's answer was not easy; the older child would serve the younger—the child of promise. She most likely knew this would break tradition and possibly lead to conflict in the family. She did not question it, instead, she fought for it at all cost. Now, Rebekah walked a slippery slope trying to ensure that her youngest son would receive his God-ordained birthright. She was not always perfect, she made mistakes along the way, but she was not afraid and God chose to use her brave, willing heart. We do not have to be perfect for God to use us. The Bible is filled with imperfect people that God used in big ways. *Thankfully, it is God that does the work in and through us, and many times in-spite of us! We are not perfect, but the perfect God in us never makes mistakes in choosing us.*

LIFE LESSONS:

1. **GENEROSITY**: In Matthew 5:41, Jesus asks us to be two-mile people in a one mile world! This is simply what Rebekah did! Serving involves physical labor, emotional output, and sacrifice of time. Laziness should never be a part of a Christians life. Serving others puts us on the road to God's blessing and God's will.

2. **GRIT**: Life will require us to have grit! Like Rebekah we must be strong, decisive, and determined to finish what we start! "I will go" are words of faith. The steps of a righteous "woman" are ordered of the Lord, but it's up to her to actually take them! It takes faith to step out into the unknown and follow God fully! Life will even require us to do the hard thing. Emotions cannot rule over our decisions in life. We must have the courage and "gumption" to follow the plan that God has chosen for us even when it is not easy. The Holy Spirit is our Helper! He will help us to have grit when we need it and temper the grit when we don't!

3. **GRACE**: Having grace and compassion when we are hurting ourselves is never easy but as our text lets us know, it is doable! We are chosen to do whatever it takes to follow God's plan! This often times means that we set aside our own pain in order to ease the pain of others. This doesn't mean that we suppress what is going on in our lives, but it gives us perspective to get out of ourselves and serve other people. In doing so, we will find that the Lord has a way of healing us while helping others. And like Rebekah, we don't always get it right, but thank God, "He giveth more grace" (James 4:6). If our heart is pure and we stay in life union with Christ, we will find that we can go boldly to the throne of grace and find mercy and grace to help us in our time of need (Hebrews 4:16).

"When you don't know what to do next, just do the thing in front of you."

-Elisabeth Elliot

Jim Elliot earned his crown at the end of a Huaorani spear in 1956. Two years later his widow, Elisabeth, their three-year-old daughter Valerie, and missionary Rachel Saint moved into the same Ecuadorian community that martyred Elliot and four colleagues. They lived in Huaorani huts and survived on barbecued monkey limbs and other local fare. They taught the Huaorani that Jesus died for their sins. Her story became a living letter to the world of what a woman "chosen to go the extra mile" looked like. In Wheaton College she concluded that she may be chosen to remain single. Less than five years after her marriage, she became a widow turned missionary. God chose her to make a mark. He chose her to keep going, one step at a time. Elisabeth passed from this life in 2015 after a ten-year battle with dementia. It is not her death that we memorialize, but the extra-ordinary, extra-mile life that has impacted us all.

Rebekah's death is never written about in scripture, only where she was buried (Genesis 23:2). The way she lived her life is what was important. It is what we read and talk about today, thousands of years later. From watering the camels to ensuring that her son Jacob received his birthright and blessing, Rebekah never shied away from the challenges she faced. It was often in mundane tasks that she impacted those around her. We are not all chosen to be like Elisabeth Elliot, nor are we all chosen to be like Rebekah, but we are chosen to keep moving forward and to go the extra mile. We do not gauge our progress by how far we've gone, but by how many we've blessed.

What do you want people to remember about your life?

Read Philippians 2:5-8.
Paul describes Jesus' perspective of His life. It is how He viewed relationships in light of His divine purpose that we are to imitate. As we are challenged to live a two-mile life, we must do so from the perspective of the cross. Christ is always our primary relationship.

With Philippian 2:5-8 in mind, use it as a guideline for the Cross graph below:

- **Put your name at the bottom of the cross,** not to be buried or crushed under its power, but tethered to its grace.
- **Then write your various relationships on either side of the cross.** You can list names or categories.

_____

"In your relationships with one another,
have the same mindset as Christ Jesus."
Philippians 2:5 NIV

We should use wisdom when making a commitment to help others. *What are three steps you can take when asked to help meet a need in someone's life?*

1.

2

3.

How has God arranged divine opportunities to get you out of your comfort zone?

When an opportunity became more than you bargained for, how did you handle it?

What have you learned from past experiences to help you better live the "two-mile" life?

Fun Facts: About Camels and Water Jars

♦ It is estimated that a camel can drink approximately 25 gallons of water each and Eliezer brought 10 camels.

♦ The average water jar in Rebekah's day held only 3 gallons of water.

With the above "Fun Fact" in mind, how many trips would Rebekah have had to take, going back and forth from the well to the trough, to provide enough water for all of the camels Eliezer brought? (yes, it is a math question.)

What are you willing to pour out of your own water pot (from your time and treasure) to care for a stranger? Write it next to the water pot below:

SCRIPTURE REFERENCES: Read Her Story!
GENESIS 22, 23; 24-27

SIGNATURE:
Rebekah [ruh-BEK-uh: meaning unknown]

SETTING:
[Date: About 1925 B.C.] Rebekah was born in Haran (modern-day south-east Turkey), a city renowned for pagan worship. In this ancient Mesopotamian land, Rebekah would have watched progress forging ahead in trade, building, and the sale of fine crafts. As the great-niece of Abraham, Rebekah must have grown up hearing family stories about Abraham leaving everything to follow God into an unknown future.

The Bible was written and lived out in cultures that were rich in hospitality and generosity. It was not uncommon for travelers to come upon a home and expect to be taken in for food and lodging. Most people would have understood what was expected of them. Even the Law of Moses made accommodation for hospitality. However, the law could only do so much. Your hands will only be as generous as your heart is toward any need. The Old Testament provides us with examples of men and women who scoffed at extending such kindnesses. Some were cruel to the point of foolishness. Once again, the scriptures remind us that a "two-mile" life cannot be legislated it must be cultivated.

Read 1 Samuel 25:1-17.
A dispute arose between David and a fool-hearted man named Nabal. David had a legitimate need and Nabal, even though he was perfectly positioned to be a blessing, crudely declined. His rejection of David's request was so offensive that David prepared a swift retaliation.

What kindness had David shown Nabal prior to his request of supplies?

How many men were "strapped with swords" following David to confront Nabal?

What was the probable outcome?

Read verses 17-35.
God's mercy was shown in the actions of Nabal's wife Abigail. She was as wise as he was foolish.

How did Abigail react when she heard what had happened?

Take an inventory of what she brought to David?

_____ Loaves of bread   _____ Wineskins full of wine   _____ Sheep
_____ Roasted grain   _____ Raisin Clusters   _____ Fig Cakes

How did Abigail react when she met David?

Because of her willingness to act quickly with humility and generosity, the situation was diffused. Later, the Lord allowed Abigail to become David's wife. God chose her to go the extra mile in this situation and her world was greatly impacted because of it.

What do you think Abigail's strongest quality was? **Circle one.**

Servant-Hearted   Wholehearted Giver

Quick Responder   Faithful in Follow-Through

Read John 12:26.
What does God promise those who show up prepared and ready to generously pour from their lives?

The stories of the Bible all lead us to one significant fact; God loves us and has equipped us with all that we need to fulfill His purposes in our lives. There is nothing that can hold us back from accomplishing our God-given purpose.

Jesus turned the world upside down. He preached a kingdom conduct that was contrary to the culture around Him. For example, the Romans believed mercy was weakness; Jesus said the merciful were blessed. For three and a half years, our Savior dismantled wrong beliefs and behaviors. In every conversation or interaction He perpetually shifted the focus to the Father. All that Jesus said and did was to show us what the Father expects of His children.

The New Testament epistles teach us how to behave by instruction. Jesus shows us how to behave by example.

Read John 13:1-14.

Jesus washed the disciples' feet. Sounds very straight forward, doesn't it? However, He was again, challenging the culture of the day. During His last opportunity to physically minister to them, He stoops to the lowest position of service. Jesus could have placed His hands on them and prayed for healing or deliverance. He might have preached one last charge. He could have held their money sacks and prayed they would never be empty. But out of all the things He might have done, He chose to *serve* them. The foot washer was the least desirable position, the lowest of the low. In one final, beautifully illustrated sermon, Christ showed us what pleases our Father most; loving each other to the point of submission, and going the extra mile.

Why did Peter refuse Jesus offer at first?

How did Jesus respond?

How might you respond in that situation?

In Verse 14, what is Jesus' final charge concerning servanthood? Write the verse out and underline His final charge.

Read John 13:16.
In this passage what was Jesus telling us about going the extra mile?

Read Matthew 5:38-44.
Complete the thought below as it pertains to this passage.

- If you get slapped on the cheek,
  _____.

- If you get sued and lose your shirt,
  _____.

- If a soldier asks you to carry his pack a mile,
  _____.

- If someone asks for something,
  _____.

- If someone want to borrow from you,
  _____.

How should you treat your enemies,

_____ ,

_____ ,

_____

_____ and _____

_____.

Each of these statements contradicted the culture and exceeded the law at the same time. Chosen one, Jesus has given you everything you need to go the extra mile. It is a lifestyle that still conflicts with our culture. People may not understand why you choose to follow Jesus in this way but leave that to the Father and keep serving anyway!

An unknown author once said, *"Your life is a gift from God to you, what you do with it is your gift to God."* Since life is a gift, consider these things as you strive to use your days wisely!

Declare this statement:

I am chosen by God!

Read the following scriptures

- *"But you are a chosen people, a royal priesthood, a holy nation, God's special possession, that you may declare the praises of Him who called you out of darkness into his wonderful light."* 1 Peter 2:9 (NIV)

- *"But now, O Jacob, listen to the LORD who created you. O Israel, the one who formed you says, "Do not be afraid, for I have ransomed you. I have called you by name; you are mine."* Isaiah 43:1 (NLT)

- *"Instead, God chose things the world considers foolish in order to shame those who think they are wise. And he chose things that are powerless to shame those who are powerful."* 1 Corinthians 1:27 (NLT)

- *"Even before he made the world, God loved us and chose us in Christ to be holy and without fault in his eyes. God decided in advance to adopt us into his own family by bringing us to himself through Jesus Christ. This is what he wanted to do, and it gave him great pleasure."* Ephesians 1:4-5 (NLT)

After reading the above Scriptures write a confession/declaration about being chosen by God. You may want to transfer this on a 3x5 card and speak it over yourself each day.

He knows your name; do you know His? God has revealed His heart in scripture through various names. When you know Him as He is known, your relationship with Him will deepen significantly.

Look up the following scriptures and draw a line to the name of God it matches.

- Genesis 22:14
- Exodus 17:15
- Exodus31:13
- Judges 6:24
- 1 Samuel 1:3, 17:45
- Psalm 23:1
- Jeremiah 23:6
- Ezekiel 48:35

Yahweh Tsidkenu: "The Lord our Righteousness."

Yahweh Nissi: "The Lord is my Banner."

YahwehRo'i: "The Lord my Shepherd."

Jireh (Yireh): "The Lord will provide."

Yahweh Shammah: "The Lord is there."

Yahweh Maccaddeshcem: "The Lord your Sanctifier."

Yahweh Sabbaoth: "The Lord of Hosts."

Yahweh Shalom: "The Lord is Peace."

"What shall we say about such wonderful things as these? If God is for us, who can ever be against us?"
Romans 8:31 (NLT)

SIMPLIFY: Personal Application

Without a doubt the story of Rebekah watering the camels has been presented as inspiration to young women for many generations. She had the character of a doer, and not just a talker. She was strong, decisive, and determined to finish what she started. She was chosen to exceed expectations; to go above and beyond the call of duty. Rebekah was not one to sit on the sidelines.

Choose one thing that you know you could do more than the bare minimum in. Is there an opportunity for you to surpass expectations in caring for your home and family or in your place of employment, or for a stranger?

SUPPLICATION: Prayer Focus

Father, You are the God of Rebekah and I am heir to the promises that You brought through her life. You know me completely and You equip, anoint, and give me favor in all that I do. I surrender fully to Your plans. Help me to be quick to respond to Your voice so that I do not miss any appointments or assignments that You have for me. I have been chosen to go the extra mile. Lord, grant me the grace to live a life of excellence, to give my all in whatever I am called to do. My desire is to hear, "Well Done Good & Faithful Servant.
Amen.

STORY BOARD: Journal Notes

What was revealed to you about the Character of God through HER STORY?

I AM:

Loved

Worthy

Chosen

Redeemed

EMPOWERED

Equipped

Treasured

Daughter of the King

Chosen

FOR THE
IMPOSSIBLE!

HER STORY

Mary, the Mother of Jesus

By Ashley Sharp

*"Now in the sixth month the angel Gabriel was sent by God to a city of Galilee named Nazareth, to a virgin betrothed to a man whose name was Joseph, of the house of David. The virgin's name was Mary. And having come in, the angel said to her, "... Do not be afraid, Mary, for you have found favor with God. And behold, you will conceive in your womb and bring forth a Son and shall call His name Jesus. He will be great and will be called the Son of the Highest; ...Then Mary said to the angel, "How can this be, since I do not know a man?" And the angel answered and said to her, "...**For with God nothing will be impossible**."*

LUKE 1:26-37 (NKJV)

Can you imagine being a young teen in Mary's shoes? I think back on my own life at that age. I always felt the call to ministry. I was sixteen when the Lord confirmed that call through a prophecy. My parents had just divorced, many people walked out of my life, and I was unsure of where I belonged.

Living in a small town, I had no one to mentor or help me. This call seemed *impossible*. It wasn't a call to birth the Savior, but it was a call to something that I felt was impossible. I chose to believe that if God called me to it, He would bring it to pass. Since then, God sent pastors into my life, Melissa and Jimmy Patillo, that have become parents and mentors. As I began to step into ministry, God brought that prophecy back to mind with 1 Thessalonians 5:24 (NKJV), *"He who calls you is faithful, who also will do it."* I have tried to be obedient to the call and have seen many parts of that prophecy unfold. As we look at the life of Mary, examine your own life. Does it seem that God has called you to the *impossible*? Maybe you feel too young, too old, or too inadequate. However, we can't base our life on *feelings*. God may call us to things that *seem* impossible, but *"With God nothing is impossible!"* J.C. Maxwell said it like this, *"What may be an impossibility for us is merely an opportunity for God."*

> ## It may have seemed impossible, but Mary chose to submit to the call and believe the Word of the Lord.

THE SITUATION

Because of her young age, questionable hometown, low financial and social statuses, it would seem unlikely that God would use her. Yet, God chose her for one of the greatest calls that anyone would ever receive. She was to give birth to His son. Mary's situation was not going to be an easy one. There would be talk, scandal, her fiancé could divorce her, and she could be stoned to death. Yet, when Gabriel appeared to her, he said, *"Rejoice, highly favored one, the Lord is with you; blessed are you among women!"* She was troubled at these words. Who wouldn't be? He goes on to say, *"be not afraid,"* and *again* states that she was *"favored."* The Greek word for *favored* means *"clothed with grace."* In other words, the Lord would give her grace to do what He called her to do! He said that she would conceive a son and she was to call Him Jesus. Mary then questioned Gabriel, "how can this be, I do not know a man?" He explained to Mary how she would conceive. Her response was, *"Be it unto me according to thy word."* It was a response of faith! It may have seemed impossible, but Mary chose to submit to the call and believe the Word of the Lord.

THE CONFIRMATION

Next, we see the confirmation of the call, in Luke 1:39-45. Mary went to her cousin Elizabeth's house. When Mary greeted her, the baby leaped in Elizabeth's womb, and she was filled with the Holy Spirit. Elizabeth said with a loud voice, *"Blessed are you among women, and blessed is the fruit of your womb! But why is this granted to me, that the mother of my Lord should come to me? For indeed, as soon as the voice of your greeting sounded in my ears, the babe leaped in my womb for joy. Blessed is she who believed, for there will be a fulfillment of those things which were told her from the Lord."* The Lord confirmed His word to Mary through Elizabeth. Because of Mary's response of faith, even in the face of all of the impossibilities, she was now going to see the fulfillment of the Word of the Lord.

THE EXALTATION

Mary began to magnify the Lord for what He was about to do through her! To *"magnify"* means *"to rejoice or praise."* She hadn't seen the fulfillment, yet she praised Him in advance! This too was a response of faith. Mary magnified the Lord because she believed *"with God nothing was impossible!"* The New Living Translation says it like this, *"for the Word of God will never fail."* That means whatever God says, He will do! Through this small-town girl, God was about to birth the Savior of the world! Not only would there be generational impact, but the world would also never be the same! The salvation of man, healing of sickness, and deliverance were all connected to her submission to the call.

LIFE LESSONS:

1. **THE SITUATION:** Mary's life should be an encouragement to us today. God can use the impossibilities of our lives as an opportunity to show His power! It doesn't matter what your life looks like or where you came from. It doesn't matter how young or how old you are. If God can use Mary, the young, poor, small-town girl that she was, He can use you regardless of your situation! We must always remember that *"He who calls us is faithful"* (1 Thessalonians 5:24 NKJV). It may be a call beyond what we can comprehend, but our situation does not limit God! We must be like Mary and respond to His call in faith and submission! Remember, if He calls us to it, He will grace us to do it!

2. **THE CONFIRMATION**: Just like God confirmed His Word to Mary through Elizabeth, He will confirm His Word to you. There are many ways for you to receive confirmation. God may use Scripture, a sermon, or even a prophecy (*as He did in my life*) to let you know you're on track. The possibilities of confirmation are endless. Regardless of the method, rest assured, there will always be confirmation. Elizabeth told Mary, *"Blessed is she who believed, for there will be a fulfillment of those things which were told her from the Lord."* When God confirms His Word, you can rest assured that the fulfillment of that Word is on its way!

3. **THE EXALTATION**: Mary not only chose to believe God, but she also began to *praise Him in advance* for what He was about to do through her! Notice, she didn't keep questioning the call. She didn't wrestle with doubt. She simply praised Him for it! Praising God, before we see the impossible become possible, is an act of faith! God responds to faith! Choose to praise the Lord in the face of every impossibility that surrounds you. Choose to praise Him when the confirmations come! Choose to praise Him before you see His plans for your life come to pass! While you're waiting for God to open the door, go ahead and praise Him in the hallway!

If He calls us to it, He will grace us to do it!

YOUR STORY: Personal Reflection

Chosen woman, God has designed you for a specific purpose. It doesn't matter where you find yourself in life, where you came from, or what circumstances surround you. His plans for you are great! You must not let your past dictate your future! As you reflect on your life through these questions, remember, no matter how impossible your call seems God can take what's *impossible* and make it *possible* for you!

How would you have felt when you were 12-16 years old in Mary's shoes?

The teen years are complicated to say the least. It's a time in life when peer pressure is the strongest. The pressure to conform to the world is enormous.

Emotions and hormones make life a roller coaster. These were the years that Mary submitted herself to the plan of God to see the impossible become possible. However, we can respond in obedience to the call on our lives no matter our age. We must follow the Shepherd not the herd!

It doesn't matter your age, whether younger or older, there are people in your life that you can impact. Chosen woman, you can make a difference! **Think about those around you and fill out the following:**

WHO CAN I BE AN EXAMPLE TO?	HOW CAN I BE AN EXAMPLE?

Who has had an impact on your life?

Elizabeth was an encourager and a positive influence in Mary's life. God sends people into our lives to mentor, train, and pull out the gifts that are on the inside of us. Every one of us are where we are today because someone obeyed the call of God on their life. Just like our lives would not be the same without their obedience, our obedience will impact others. Be obedient! Someone's eternal destiny depends on it. Napoleon Hill once said, *"Think twice before you speak, because your words and influence will plant the seed of either success or failure in the mind of another."*

Do you feel that God has called you to something that seems impossible? If so, what?

Have you felt that your situation limits God's ability to use you?

Hard times in life can become the greatest testimonies of God's faithfulness. God doesn't change His mind because of our circumstances. He already knew His plan for you before you were ever formed in your mother's womb. Purpose precedes production. You are no accident. Your existence hasn't taken God by surprise. He doesn't ask that we figure things out on our own, He simply wants us to trust that He already has.

Have you been afraid to respond to the call because you have felt inadequate?

You can't change where you started, but you can change the direction you are going!

In what ways has God confirmed His call on your life?

Have you already seen God move through you because you responded in faith and obeyed the call on your life? If so, how?

"What may be an *impossibility* for us, is merely an opportunity for God."

J.C. Maxwell

SCRIPTURE REFERENCE: Read Her Story!
Matthew 1; 2; 12:46-50; 13:55; Mark 3:31-35; Luke 1; 2; 8:19-20; John 2:1-11; 7:5; 19:25-27; Acts 1:14

SIGNATURE:
MARY [MAIR-ee: "Loved by Yahweh"]— Mother of Jesus

SETTING:
[Date: 5 B.C.] Mary, the mother of Jesus, was from a small village in Galilee called Nazareth. Mary was a peasant girl. She was not well known, nor was she rich. She was simply a humble, small-town girl. The custom of the day was for girls to marry young. Many commentators say that Mary could have been between the ages of twelve and sixteen when Gabriel appeared to her.

Mary's situation may have *seemed* impossible, but her *response of faith* is what God needed in order to make the impossible possible! The Bible states, *"Nothing is impossible with God!"* The supernatural power of God is God's response, to man's response, to God's initiative!

Look up the following scriptures and fill in the blanks.

- *"For _____ _____ nothing is impossible."* **LUKE 1:37 (NKJV)**

- *"But Jesus looked at them and said to them,"With men this is_____ , but_____ _____ ___ _____ are possible."* **MATTHEW 19:26 (NKJV)**

- *"But Jesus _____ ____ _____ and said, "With men it is_____, but not with God; for with God _____ _____ _____ _____."* **MARK 10:27 (NKJV)**

Read Psalm 37:5 (NKJV).

*"**Commit** your way to the Lord, trust also in Him, and He will bring it to pass."*

According to *The International Standard Bible Encyclopedia:*

"TO *COMMIT*" means *"To Entrust."*

Because Mary committed her way to the Lord, she saw the fulfillment of God's call on her life. She chose to *"entrust"* herself to God. She responded in faith when she said, *"Be it unto me according to thy word."* She didn't say, *"Well Gabriel, let me think about it."* She didn't consult with her friends or parents first. She didn't even consult with her fiancé. She didn't weigh out what could happen before she agreed to it. Mary knew the Lord was calling her and she willingly stepped out in faith and obedience.

Just like Mary, when the Lord calls, our response should be, *"Be it unto me according to thy word."* Many times, people try to know every detail of what their life will be if they say yes to God, instead of trusting Him in humble submission. Remember, yieldedness is the path to fruitfulness.

The following were ordinary men, but God used all of them to write the sacred scriptures as they were moved on by the Holy Ghost *(2 Peter 1:21).*

- **Moses** was an orphan yet became the great deliverer of Israel and withstood Pharaoh.
- **Nehemiah** was a cupbearer to the king yet became the catalyst in rebuilding Jerusalem after the Babylonian exile.
- **David** was a shepherd boy who became the greatest king in Israel's history who fought many battles along the way.
- **Amos** was a farmer whose prophetic writings foretold of the destruction of the northern kingdom of Israel and teaches us today that God will judge injustice.
- **Peter, James and John** were fishermen, yet they were chosen by Jesus and walked with Him throughout His earthly ministry. Later, they were pillars in the church and were in the upper room on the Day of Pentecost to receive the Baptism in the Holy Spirit. Their sacred writings are part of our Bible today!

God also used these ordinary women to do extraordinary things in their generations.

- **Shiphra and Puuah** were ordinary midwives to the Hebrew women in Egypt who went against the order of Pharaoh to abort the male children and helped protect the progeny of the Hebrews. As a result, God gave them their own land.
- **Esther** was an orphan who God used to stand against the wicked plots of Haman and save her nation for perpetuity.
- **Dorcas (Tabitha)** was a seamstress who was merciful to the poor. She was raised from the dead by the Apostle Peter and because of her many people in Joppa believed.

If God used all of these people, then what is our excuse? He can use us no matter who we are or what our situation may be. *If you think you're too small to make a difference, try sleeping with a mosquito!*

What would the world look like today if every believer stepped out in faith and obedience to the call of God on their life regardless of their circumstances, what people say, or what they may have to face?

If you live for the praise of people, you will die by their criticism!

After the Lord confirmed His word to Mary, we see another act of faith, *she began to magnify the Lord*. Her response of praise *before the fulfillment* looks a lot like what happened when God spoke to Abram.

Read Romans 4:18-22.

How did Abram respond to God?

"*Contrary to hope, in hope believed*" means, despite the *hopelessness* and *impossibility* of Abram's situation, He chose to believe God. He knew that He who promised was able to bring it to pass! Verse 20 states that Abram, "*Did not waver at the promise of God.*" He didn't doubt the promise of God. Had Abram looked around at his circumstances and considered all the things that were not in his favor, it may have not been so easy to believe God. He may have doubted. But Abram didn't look *around.* He looked *up* and chose to believe God! And as an act of faith, Abram began to *praise* God before the promise was fulfilled! Abram and Mary both responded in faith before their promises were fulfilled!

Praise is a response of faith. Faith requires corresponding action. Faith without works is dead, and dead faith doesn't produce living results!

Dead faith doesn't produce living results!

Look up the following scriptures and fill in the blanks by answering the following question:

How can we praise God?

- *By_____ up your _____. (Psalm 134:2)*
- *By _____ praises to God. (Psalm 147:1; 100:2)*
- *With your _____. (Hebrews 13:15)*
- *With _____ and _____. (Psalm 149:3)*
- *In _____ with other _____. (Hebrews 2:12)*

When we praise, the gates of heaven open, and God enters the scene. Praise prepares the way for the miraculous to happen in our lives. Mary and Abram were not the only ones to praise God before they saw the promise come to pass, we see many times in scripture where people praised God and as a result the impossible happened.

The impossible happens when people praise. **Here are a few examples: Look up the following scriptures and fill in the boxes:**

Scripture	What Were Their Circumstances?	What Was The Result of Their Praise?
Acts 16:16-26 (Paul and Silas)		
2 Chronicles 20:14-22 (King Jehoshaphat)		
1 Samuel 1:1-21 (Hannah)		

Each of these people were in the midst of impossible situations. As a result of their praise, God was able to take the impossible and make it possible in their lives. Their praise was an act of faith!

Have you responded in faith to a promise from God and saw it fulfilled in your life? Explain.

Are you still standing in faith for the fulfillment of a promise? If so, what Scripture are you standing on?

If you're still waiting, remember that the fulfillment was not immediate in Mary or in Abram's life. They stood in faith until they saw the promises of God come to fruition! Chosen woman, continue to stand in faith, being obedient to what He has told you to do. When you do, you will see God take what's impossible in your life and make it possible! If God could close the lions mouth for Daniel, part the red sea for Moses, make the sun stand still for Joshua, open the prison for Peter, put a baby in the arms of Sarah, and raise Lazarus from the dead, nothing you are facing today is too hard for Him to handle!

Match these impossible situations with their miraculous outcome to increase your faith! Remember, God is no respecter of persons (Romans 2:11). What He did for them, He can do for you!

Harsh Slavery of Egypt	_____	A. Jesus says, "Receive your sight."
Giant Goliath's Murderous Threats	_____	B. Forgiveness of an adulteress.
Hungry Lion's Den	_____	C. Jesus cries, "Lazarus come forth."
Stoning to Death	_____	D. Jesus has compassion and says, "Young man arise."
Blinded Beggar	_____	E. Oil multiplies in borrowed vessels.
Dead Brother	_____	F. Dry path in the midst of the Red Sea.
Dead Son	_____	G. Accurate sling shot of David to the forehead.
Insurmountable Debt of a widow	_____	H. God shuts the mouths

"A MIRACLE" =

"God doing for us what we cannot do ourselves!"

Fun Facts: About Mary

- To be chosen as the mother of the long awaited Messiah—to give birth to the deliverer of God's people— would be the highest calling imaginable for a woman of any century, but even more dramatically so for a woman of first century Israel. Yet, God chose to place that high honor on a poor, socially insignificant, unmarried young virgin named Mary.

- According to many commentators, Nazareth was only 40,000 square meters which is a little less than 10 acres. In Jesus' time the population of Nazareth was estimated to be between 200-500 people.

- In Mary and Joseph's day, marriages were arranged by the parents of the bride and groom, many times without consulting them. A contract was prepared in which the grooms parents paid a bride price. This deemed the couple married although the actual ceremony and consummation of the marriage may not occur for one year to many years down the road. The betrothal period was often a test of fidelity. Should infidelity occur during the betrothal period, the groom could divorce his betrothed.

- In her pregnancy, Mary risked much more than a damaged reputation. She risked her very life. According to the law, a Jewish woman who failed to remain a virgin before marriage could be stoned to death (see Deut. 22:20-21).

- Mary traveled somewhere between 80-100 miles from Galilee to the hill country of Judea to visit Elizabeth in Luke chapter 1. She was already with child on this journey!

- Mary's Magnificat resembles *Hannah's song* in 1 Samuel 2:1-10, but also has at least 12 other allusions to the Old Testament. This means that Mary was a woman who studied and knew God's Word. The Scriptures were on her heart and came out through her song!

SIMPLIFY: Personal Application

Because Mary yielded to God, He was able to bring His Son into the world. She sang His praises for choosing her to bring forth the promised Savior of the world.

"And Mary said:
my soul glorifies the Lord
and my spirit rejoices in God my Savior,
for He has been mindful
of the humble state of his servant.
from now on all
generations will call
me blessed."
LUKE 1:46-48

What is God wanting to bring to pass in the earth through your yielding?

Sometimes God will ask us to do something we don't understand and the only way to fully understand is to obey. Naaman learned a valuable lesson: **to understand why, submit and apply!** Don't hold back or dismiss God's call on your life because of your situation. Just like there were other people whose destinies were linked to the call on Mary's life, you too have a call where people are linked to your obedience! Someone somewhere is depending on you to obey God! Chosen woman, trust the Lord in the face of every impossibility that surrounds you and allow Him to use you for His glory! What is one area in your life today where the Lord has clearly spoken, that you can choose obedience and show His glory? You've been chosen for the impossible!

Repeat this often...

"My impossibilities are simply **God's opportunities!"**

SUPPLICATION: Prayer Focus

Father, I come to You in the name of Jesus through the power of the Holy Spirit. I thank You for the call You have placed on my life. You have chosen me for a specific purpose. I choose to be obedient to that call and I choose to be obedient to Your voice. I will trust You no matter how impossible the situation may seem because I know that every impossibility is an opportunity for You to move. I want Your will for my life, not my own. So, I choose today to submit my life to You. Use me for Your glory.

In Jesus name, Amen.

STORY BOARD: Journal Notes

What was revealed to you about the Character of God through HER STORY?

"BUT **YOU** ARE GOD'S *CHOSEN* TREASURE, PRIESTS WHO ARE KINGS, A SPIRITUAL NATION SET APART AS GOD'S DEVOTED ONES. HE CALLED **YOU** OUT OF DARKNESS TO EXPERIENCE HIS MARVELOUS LIGHT, AND NOW HE CLAIMS **YOU** AS HIS VERY OWN."

- 1 PETER 2:9 TPT

WORSHIP PLAY LIST:

Chosen Songs

If you are looking for songs to go with each lesson, we have listed a few of our favorites just for you. These are beautiful songs that will create an atmosphere of worship for each session theme. You may want to download them for listening during your private time with the Lord, or you may want to use them in a worship or soaking service. Chosen woman of God, enjoy His abundant presence!

Session 1
DEBORAH: Chosen to Arise!

Song #1: I BELONG TO JESUS – BETHEL MUSIC

Song #2: THANK YOU JESUS FOR THE BLOOD – CHARITY GAYLE

Song #3: EGYPT – BETHEL MUSIC

Session 2
RUTH: Chosen to Walk it Out!

Song #1: WHO YOU SAY I AM – HILLSONG WORSHIP

Song #2: CANVAS AND CLAY – PAT BARRETT

Song #3: ALWAYS GOOD – BETHEL MUSIC HANNAH MCCLURE

Session 3
ACHSAH: Chosen to Ask for More!

Song #1: LORD, I NEED YOU – MATT MAHER

Song #2: TOO GOOD TO NOT BELIEVE – BETHEL MUSIC

Song #3: BREATHE MIRACLES – RED ROCKS WORSHIP

Session 4
WOMEN AT THE CROSS: Chosen for Perseverance!

Song #1: WAIT ON YOU – MAVERICK CITY MUSIC

Song #2: IF GOD/NOTHING BUT THE BLOOD – CASEY J

Song #3: YOU'RE GONNA BE OK – BRIAN AND JENN JOHNSON

Session 5
ISAIAH 54 MOTHER: Chosen for Spiritual Mothering!

Song #1: GOODNESS OF GOD – BETHEL MUSIC

Song #2: YOU HOLD IT ALL TOGETHER – MAVERICK CITY MUSIC

Song #3: PAIN AND GRACE – KIRBY KAPLE

Session 6

LOIS AND EUNICE: Chosen for Legacy!

Song #1: THE BLESSING – ELEVATION

Song #2: TALKING TO JESUS – ELEVATION WORSHIP AND MAVERICK CITY MUSIC

Song #3: LEAVE THIS HOUSE SINGING – WOLL REAGAN AND UNITED PURSUIT

Session 7

HANNAH: Chosen for Breakthrough!

Song #1: DO IT AGAIN – ELEVATION WORSHIP

Song #2: SOMETHING HAS TO BREAK – RED ROCKS WORSHIP

Song #3: WON'T STOP NOW – ELEVATION WORSHIP

Session 8

JAEL: Chosen for Bravery!

Song #1: DANCING ON THE WAVES – WE THE KINGDOM

Song #2: TAKE COURAGE – KRISTENE DIMARCO

Song #3: NOT AFRAID – JESUS CULTURE

Session 9

THE SAMARITAN WOMAN: Chosen to Share the Gospel!

Song #1: COME, MAKE WAY – UNVEILED WORSHIP

Song #2: COME OUT OF HIDING – STEFFANY GRETZINGER

Song #3: KING OF MY HEART – BETHEL MUSIC

Session 10

PRISCILLA: Chosen for Ministry!

Song #1: AVAILABLE – ELEVATION

Song #2: YES I WILL – VERTICAL WORSHIP

Song #3: REFINER – MAVERICK CITY MUSIC

Session 11

REBEKAH: Chosen to Go the Extra Mile!

Song #1: NEVER WALK ALONE – HILLSONG WORSHIP

Song #2: GRAVES INTO GARDENS – ELEVATION WORSHIP

Song #3: MOVE YOUR HEART – UPPERROOM

Session 12

MARY: Chosen for the Impossible!

Song #1: YES (OBEDIENCE) – DAVID AND NICOLE BINION

Song #2: I GIVE MYSELF AWAY – WILLIAM MCDOWEL

Song #3: MADE A WAY – TRAVIS GREENE

Song #4: MARY DID YOU KNOW– PENTATONIX

EMPOWERED WOMEN'S MINISTRIES

connection

I-Connect provides the opportunity for PCG women to join hearts and hands with **Empowered Women's Ministries**. We value your voice in our community of faith and your desire to help us as we advance the Kingdom of God **together as one.**

Send $5.00 for a one year membership, along with your name and email, to your local church, district, or to Empowered Women's Ministries 2701 Brown Trail, Bedford TX 76021

AN EMPOWERED CONNECT MEMBERSHIP PROVIDES:

- A full one-year membership.
- A one-year monthly subscription to our "Empower Her" e-newsletter filled with empowering articles, Scripture focus, outreach projects, and much more.
- Prayer from your local, district and national leaders.
- Discounts on PCG national and district designated resources, retreats, and conferences.
- Support help for furthering ministry to women in the local church and around the world.
- A connected voice and sisterhood with thousands of other Pentecostal Church of God women around the country.

LEADERS NOTES:

Chapter 1- DEBORAH

- **GIVE A TOKEN: A HEART CLIP**

  You may want to present each of your students with a heart clip as a reminder to ARISE with the gifts that God has set in your heart. (Available through Empowered Women's Ministries. See page 215).

- **RECOMMENDATIONS:**

  - Watch the movie "Harriet," about Harriet Tubman, a Deborah in her time.

  - Meet Claudia Koenig, a Deborah of our time. This is her website, Soul Savior. This is a precious one who has finished her course on this earth in 2021. Visit her website of sharing stories of leading people to the Lord as a daily lifestyle of God's love. http://www.soulsaviour.org/salvation-stories/

  - Worship with this song: *Rest on Us* Maverick City Worship Upper Room (You Tube).

  - Encourage a daily devotional book like: "Waiting on God", Andrew Murray daily readings, make this a daily habit.

Chapter 3- ACHSAH

- **GIVE A TOKEN: A Charm**

  ACHSAH's Name means "Ankle Bracelet or Tinkling ornament"- Her father undoubtedly knew when she was coming by the sound she made. Provide each woman in the group with an ankle bracelet or charm to represent Achsah's name as a reminder that we are God's daughters and God delights when we pray Big Bold prayers. (Charms are available through Empowered Women's Ministries. See page 215).

Chapter 5- ISAIAH 54 MOTHER

- **BOOK RECOMMENDATIONS**
  - *"Adorned: Living Out the Beauty of the Gospel Together"* Nancy DeMoss Wolgemuth
  - *"Passing It On"* Myles Munroe
  - *"Mentoring 101"* John Maxwell
  - *"Doctrines of the Bible"* Myer Pearlman
  - *"Qualified"* Tony Cooke
  - *"Spiritual Leadership"* J. Oswald Sanders
  - *"Celebration of Discipline"* Richard J. Foster

Chapter 6– LOIS & EUNICE

♦ **BOOK RECOMMENDATIONS**

- *"In Search of Timothy"* Tony Cooke

Chapter 9- SAMARITAN WOMAN

♦ **GIVE A TOKEN: A HEART CLIP**
If you did not give a heart clip token to your group at the close of the chapter one study, you may still want to present each of your students with a heart clip at the end of this study. Share a heart clip that reads *"YOU ARE LOVED"* as a simple reminder that you are loved by God in a great way. (Available through Empowered Women's Ministries. See page 215).

♦ **GIVE A TOKEN: STORY STICKER–** Share with all of the women in your group a sticker as a reminder that the Redeemed of the Lord Tell Their STORY. (Available through Empowered Women's Ministries. See sticker on pg. 215).

♦ **BOOK and MOVIE RECOMMENDATIONS**

- **For more information on how to share the Gospel: *EMPOWERED TO SHARE: EVANGELISM BOX–*** A comprehensive set of physical resources designed to equip believers to share the Gospel of Jesus Christ, by Joe Oden. Available at ***PCG.org/Resources .*** (See page 214).
- *Uninvited: Living Loved When You Feel Less Than, Left Out, and Lonely* by Lysa Terkeurst, Nelson Books.
- CHOSEN– Download the free app and watch *"THE CHOSEN"* Season One, episode eight and/or *"THE CHOSEN- EXTRAS– The Woman at the Well."*

EXTRA:

♦ **RECOMMENDED FOR DEEPER STUDY OF THE WORD:**

- **Download the Empowered Women's Ministry Bible Reading Guide: *PURSUING TRUTH.*** A free download available each month to guide the reader through the Bible in one year. Includes a monthly focus video from the Bible Project. Download at ***PCG.org/women-resources.***
- Subscribe to a free Bible App such as:
  - Youversion Bible app– This app includes Bible, Scripture plans and more.
  - *Dwell Bible app,*
  - *ReadScripture.*
  - *Courage For Life Bible.* A Bible app with all women reading the Word. The soothing voices of these women is relaxing and perfect for emotionally hurt women who may have a trigger to the sound of a mans voice.

Chosen Recipes

It's always fun to have some new recipes to share with friends and family. We have CHOSEN just a few of our "go-to" favorites for you to try. We chose a party favorite in a tasty chicken tortilla bake that is perfect for a simple dinner good enough for a family or several friends. When you're getting the girls together for a small group night try the healthy, refreshing watermelon fruit salad in the Summer time or the apple cider fall punch and apple cake in the Fall. Take our favorite yeast rolls to the next pot luck. Don't forget to treat your girl tribe, or a neighbor by sharing a perfectly yummy chocolate chip cookie.

CHICKEN TORTILLA BAKE
Serves 8

INGREDIENTS

- 3 or 4 Chicken Breasts (cooked and shredded)
- 2- 4 oz cans of Diced Green Chilies
- 2- 10 oz Cream of Chicken Soup
- ¼ C Chopped Onions
- ¼ C Green Onion (Chopped and Reserved)
- 1 Package (12 ct) Corn Tortillas
- 2 cup of Monterey Jack Cheese
- 1 cup Sour Cream
- 2 Cloves of Garlic, minced
- 1 tsp Salt
- ½ tsp Pepper

INSTRUCTIONS

1. Preheat oven to 350 F.
2. In a bowl, combine chicken, chilies, broth, sour cream, salt, and pepper to make a chicken mixture.
3. Spray a 9x13 pan with nonstick spray.
4. Cut tortillas into strips; set aside.
5. Place a small amount of chicken mixture on the bottom of the pan.
6. Lay half of the tortillas on top of that small amount and then pour half of the remainder of chicken mixture on them.
7. Spread half of the shredded cheese on top of it.
8. Then again layer tortilla strips and end with the other half of chicken mixture.
9. Place the final layer of cheese on top.
10. Top with reserved green onions.
11. Cover with aluminum foil and bake for 40 minutes or until casserole is bubbly hot.

YUMMY YEAST ROLLS
Yeilds 5-7 rolls

INGREDIENTS
- 2-2 ½ cup Flour
- 3 Tlb. Sugar
- 1 Pkg. (1/4 oz) Quick Rise Yeast Packet
- 1/ tsp. salt
- ¾ cup Warm Water
- 2 Tlb. Butter, melted

INSTRUCTIONS
1. In a large mixing bowl combine 1 ½ C flour, sugar, yeast, and salt.
2. Add water and butter.
3. Beat on medium speed for 3 minutes or until smooth.
4. Stir in enough remaining flour to form a soft dough.
5. Turn onto a well-floured surface. Knead until elastic and smooth; about 4-6 minutes.
6. Cover and let rise for 10 minutes.
7. Form into 6-7 rolls. Place into a well buttered pie dish.
8. Cover with a kitchen towel and let rise in a warm place for about 30 minutes.
9. Bake in a preheated oven at 375 for 11-14 minutes. Enjoy!

EASY FALL PUNCH
Yields 1 drink

INGREDIENTS
- Vanilla ice cream
- Apple cider
- Cinnamon

INSTRUCTIONS
1. Put vanilla ice cream into a tall glass
2. Then add cold apple cider
3. Top with a little cinnamon if desired.

EASY AND SO TASTY!

WATERMELON FRUIT SALAD

INGREDIENTS
- 4 cups Watermelon
- 1 1/2 cups Strawberries
- 1 1/2 cups Cherries (pitted)
- 1 1/2 cups Raspberries
- 2 Tbl Lime juice
- 1 1/2 tsp lime zest
- 2 Tbl Agave
- 1 Tbl fresh chopped mint

INSTRUCTIONS
1. Make Dressing first. Whisk together agave, lime juice, lime zest and fresh chopped mint.
2. Prep watermelon, cherries, raspberries and strawberries and place in a large bowl.
3. Drizzle dressing over the top and lightly toss.
4. Garnish with some torn mint. (If you are not a fan of mint, basil is a great replacement.)

WHY WE LOVE THIS RECIPE:

It is insanely refreshing, it disappears fast because everyone loves it, it is super light and can be served as a side for dinner or a healthy snack.

APPLE DAPPLE CAKE
Serves 12-16

INGREDIENTS
- 3 Eggs
- 1 ¼ Cups Oil
- 2 tsp. Vanilla
- 2 Cups Sugar
- 2 ¾ Cups Flour
- 1 tsp Salt
- 1 tsp Baking Soda
- 1 tsp Ground Cinnamon
- ¼ tsp Nutmeg
- ¼ Cup Flour
- 1 Cups Apples, Chopped
- 1 Cup Nuts, Chopped
- 1 Cup Coconut

TOPPING:
- 1/3 Cup Butter
- 1 Cup Brown Sugar
- ¼ Cup Milk
- 1 tsp Vanilla

INSTRUCTIONS
1. Preheat oven to 375 F.
2. Beat the eggs well. Add oil, vanilla, and sugar, beating well.
3. Sift together and add; 2 ¼ C. flour, baking soda, salt, cinnamon, and nutmeg.
4. Mix together ¼ C. flour with apples and nuts, and then fold in.
5. Pour into a greased Bundt pan and bake for approximately 70 minutes.
6. While it is baking, mix together in a saucepan the topping ingredients.
7. Boil for 2-3 minutes.
8. Pour hot topping over cake about 5 minutes after removing cake from the oven.

"This cake is a family favorite every time!
The caramel topping makes it extra delicious!"

- Kathy Whited

209

CHOCOLATE CHIP COOKIES
Yields 6 dozen cookies

These can be made ahead of time and froze for quick, fresh cookies later. You can bake a dozen at a time or just a couple for a snack. What a treat to always have these available! Simply make the dough, scoop into balls and flash freeze on a cookie sheet for approximately 30 minutes. Then you can place them into a freezer plastic bag and keep for up to 2 months.

INGREDIENTS
- 1 Cup butter (softened)
- 1 Cup Brown Sugar
- 1 Cup granulated sugar
- 2 Eggs
- 2 tsp Vanilla
- 4 Cups Flour
- 1 tsp Baking Soda
- 1 tsp salt
- ¼ Cup Milk
- 1 Bag of Chocolate Chips

INSTRUCTIONS
1. Preheat oven to 350 F.
2. Cream together the butter and the sugars thoroughly.
3. Add eggs and vanilla, beating until fluffy.
4. Mix separately the dry ingredients and add alternately with the milk.
5. Lastly, stir in the chocolate chips.
6. Bake for 10 minutes. Cookies may seem slightly undercooked, but you do not want to overcook them. Place on a cooling sheet to cool completely.

NOTE: I use a small scoop with this recipe. You can use a larger scoop and adjust your time accordingly.

* This recipe comes from Author Esther H. Shank in her book, Mennonite Country- Style Kitchen Recipes & Secrets (1987, 159).

EMPOWERED GIVING:

Alabaster Box Project

The Alabaster Box Ministry is a means of encouraging each woman to cultivate an intimate relationship with God through prayer, praise, and plentiful giving. When women pour out their offerings, they are giving back to God out of a heart of worship. Alabaster funds support the national Women's Ministries of the Pentecostal Church of God and help provide for its many out reach projects that are making a difference to a world in need.

Some of our outreach projects include:

GIRL *Talk*

RESCUE HER

IMPACT APPALACHIA

AHIKAM
Guatemala Orphanage

And much more:

- Pastors Kids of Deceased Parents
- Missionaries Worldwide
- Resource and Leadership Development

TO GIVE: pcg.org/giving.
Please click Ministries and give to Women's Ministries/Alabaster

Just as Mary took her alabaster box filled with costly oil and anointed the feet of Jesus, we too can give our best to show our love for Christ.

OTHER EMPOWERED RESOURCES:

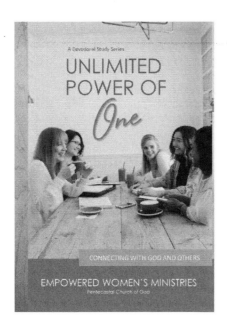

UNLIMITED: POWER OF ONE
(Connecting with God and Others)

A devotional study on connecting with God and others. Watch the unlimited power of God unfold when we unite our hearts and minds together as ONE with God through understanding:

- Who God is
- Who we are in God
- How we can represent God to the World

Book 1 of 3 in the "ONE" devotional study series.
Soft cover, 135 pages; Released 2019

$12.99

UNRIVALED: PASSION OF ONE
(Learning to Live Loved in God)

In this devotional study, discover the passionate love of God, a redefined true love that is completely unrivaled and unequal to any earthly love. While taking a deeper look in Scripture, learn what it looks like to LIVE LOVED. Together we will understand:

- We are passionately Loved by God
- We can fully trust in the Love of God
- We can passionately Live Loved to the world

Book 2 of 3 in the "ONE" devotional study series.
Soft cover, 173 pages; Released 2020

Also available in SPANISH
SIN RIVALIDAD: LA PASION DE UNO

$12.99

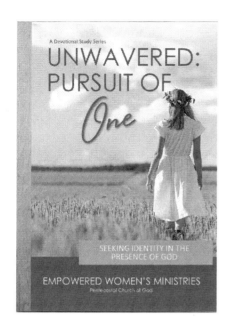

UNWAVERED: PURSUIT OF ONE

(Seeking Identity in the Presence of God)

In this devotional we will discover that our identities are not found in a life position and that the opinions of others cannot inform us of who we really are. Instead, true identity is and can only be found in relationship with God the Father. Throughout the 12 study sessions included, you will be challenged to seek God's Presence and discover the biblical truths that stand in contradiction to cultural lies— truths that unveil:

- Who we are in Jesus
- Who He created us to be
- And how we are relentlessly and unwaveringly pursued by Him

Book 3 of 3 in the "ONE" devotional study series.
Soft cover, 175 pages; Released 2021

$12.99

WHAT READERS ARE SAYING:

I totally love having tools that make our ministry role more effective and, honestly, a little easier. My goal was never to just have a 'chat time,' but, instead, to have times of connecting that would challenge women of all ages from our church to see things different. To have them believe and dream again so they can live more than a "getting by" mentality. These devotionals are a great tool in accomplishing those goals. I'm amazed at how these studies speak to our current season.

Susan Dawn Coffman– Co-pastor of Echoes From Calvary
Salinas, California

TO PURCHASE COPIES:

PCG.org/women (Resources)
empoweredwmin@pcg.org or 817-554-5900 ext. 370
PCG.org/resources
Amazon.com

Pentecostal Church
of God Resources

amazon

POSTERS-

Each poster comes printed on quality cardstock with cardboard backing and comes with plastic covering.

5x7 CHOSEN WITH A
PURPOSE/SCRIPTURE

$3.00 each

8x10 CHOSEN WITH A
PURPOSE/SCRIPTURE

$5.00 each

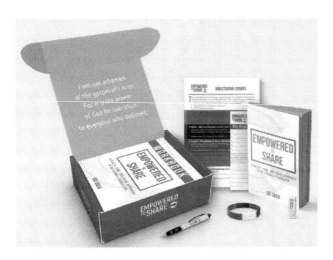

" I am not ashamed of the gospel of Christ. For it is the power of God for salvation to everyone who believes."

EVANGELISM BOX-

For more information on how to share the Gospel: *EMPOWERED TO SHARE: EVANGELISM BOX*– A comprehensive set of physical resources designed to equip believers to share the Gospel of Jesus Christ, by Joe Oden.

Includes:

- Book
- Workbook
- Flash drive
- My Five Bookmark
- Wrist band and guide

$100.00 USD

For more details or to purchase:
PCG.org/Resources

CLIPS– YOU ARE LOVED

Each clip is red with white letters reading "YOU ARE LOVED." Great as a small gift to use as a bookmark in your favorite Empowered Devotional. Perfect as a reminder to women that they are loved. Use with devotional *HER STORY: CHOSEN*—(Chp. 1 DEBORAH, Chp.; 9 THESAMARITAN WOMAN or with *UNRIVALED:PASSION OF ONE, Live Loved in God.*)

$10.00 per pack of 50 =($.20 each)
(comes in small plastic jar)
$6.25 per pack of 25 =($.25 each)
$3.00 per pack of 10 =($.30 each)
$.35 each

CHARMS-

Silver charms- perfect for group gifts. Give as a reminder to pray bold prayers along with the reading of the devotional- HER STORY: CHOSEN, (chapter 1– ACHSAH-Who's names means "Trinket, anklet ornament.")

Packet of 10 Charms $12.50

Or $1.50 each

STICKER-

Beautifully designed heavy duty waterproof sticker with "Let *the Redeemed of the Lord Tell Their Story*" Scripture. Give as a reminder to Tell the Story with "HER STORY: CHOSEN, (chapter 9– The Samaritan Woman.

$1.50 Each or for 10 or more $1.00 each

Resources Available at:
Empowered Women's Ministries
PCG.org/women (tab- Resources)
empoweredwmin@pcg.org or 817-554-5900 ext. 370
PCG.org/resources

EMPOWERED WOMEN'S MINISTRIES:

Empowered Women's Ministries is an active ministry of dedicated women of the Pentecostal Church of God. Thousands of women are inspired and motivated by the ministry through prayer, support, and outreach endeavors.

The women's ministry operates under the organizational structure of the Pentecostal Church of God on local church, state/district, national, and international levels.

Empowered Women's Ministries exist to represent Jesus Christ throughout the earth. By the power of the Holy Spirit, our mission is to EMPOWER, ENCOURAGE, and EQUIP women to live the Empowered life in Christ.

TO FIND OUT MORE ABOUT
EMPOWERED WOMEN'S MINISTRIES
AND THE PENTECOSTAL CHURCH OF GOD
CHECK OUT

pcg.org/women

FOLLOW @empoweredwomensministries on

empowered
WOMEN'S MINISTRIES
PENTECOSTAL CHURCH OF GOD

FOR ORDER INFORMATION, PLEASE VISIT
pcg.org/women
or contact us at
empoweredwmin@pcg.org
817-554-5900 ext. 370

Made in United States
Orlando, FL
09 January 2022

13186655R00120